LEISURE THE BASIS OF CULTURE

JOSEF PIEPER

LEISURE
THE BASIS OF CULTURE

translated by
ALEXANDER DRU

with an introduction by
T. S. ELIOT

PANTHEON BOOKS INC.
NEW YORK

ORIGINAL GERMAN TITLES:
Musse und Kult
and
Was heisst Philosophieren?

First Printing: January 1952
Second Printing: June 1954
Third Printing: November 1955
Fourth Printing: June 1958
Fifth Printing: February 1960

CONTENTS

LEISURE THE BASIS OF CULTURE

THE PHILOSOPHICAL ACT

CONTENTS

INTRODUCTION BY T. S. ELIOT

The complaint is frequently heard that our time has little to boast of in the way of philosophy. Whether this deficiency is due to some ailment of philosophy itself, or to the diversion of able philosophical minds towards other studies, or simply to a shortage of philosophers, is never made clear: these are divisions of the question which are apt to become confused. Certainly, 'Where are the great philosophers?' is a rhetorical question often asked by those who pursued their philosophical studies forty or fifty years ago. Allowing for the possibility that the great figures of our youth have become magnified by the passage of time, and for the probability that most of those who ask the question have not followed modern philosophical developments very closely, there remains some justification of the lament. It may be merely a longing for the appearance of a philosopher whose writings, lectures and personality will arouse the imagination as Bergson, for instance, aroused it forty years ago; but it may be also the expression of a need for philosophy in an older meaning of the word – the need for new authority to express *insight* and *wisdom*.

To those who pine for philosophy in this ampler sense, logical positivism is the most conspicuous object

11

of censure. Certainly, logical positivism is not a very nourishing diet for more than the small minority which has been conditioned to it. When the time of its exhaustion arrives, it will probably appear, in retrospect, to have been for our age the counterpart of surrealism : for as surrealism seemed to provide a method of producing works of art without imagination so logical positivism seems to provide a method of philosophizing without insight and wisdom. The attraction which it thus offers to the immature mind may have unfortunate results for some of those who pursue their undergraduate studies under its influence. Yet I believe that in the longer view, logical positivism will have proved of service by explorations of thought which we shall, in future, be unable to ignore; and even if some of its avenues turn out to be blind alleys, it is, after all, worth while exploring a blind alley, if only to discover that it *is* blind. And, what is more important for my theme, I believe that the sickness of philosophy, an obscure recognition of which moves those who complain of its decline, has been present too long to be attributable to any particular contemporary school of thought.

At the time when I myself was a student of philosophy – I speak of a period some thirty-five to forty years ago – the philosopher was beginning to suffer from a feeling of inferiority to the exact scientist. It was felt that the mathematician was the man best qualified to philosophize. Those students of philosophy who had not come to philosophy from mathematics did their best (at least, in the university in which my studies were conducted) to try to become imitation mathematicians – at least to the extent of acquainting themselves with the paraphernalia of symbolic logic. (I remember one enthusiastic contemporary who devised a Symbolic Ethics, for which he had to invent several symbols not found in the *Principia Mathematica*.) Beyond this, some familiarity with contemporary physics and with contemporary biology was also prized: a philosophical argument supported by illustrations from one of these sciences was more respectable than one which lacked them – even if the supporting evidence was sometimes irrelevant. Now I am quite aware that to the philosopher no field of knowledge should come amiss. The ideal philosopher would be at ease with every science, with every branch of art, with every language, and with the whole of human history. Such encyclopaedic knowledge might preserve him from excessive awe of those disciplines in which he was untrained, and excessive bias towards those in which he was well exercised. But in an age in which every branch of study becomes more subdivided and specialized, the ideal of omniscience is more and more remote from realization. Yet only omniscience is enough, once the philosopher begins to rely upon science. No one today, I imagine, would follow the example of Bosanquet, who in his *Logic* leant so heavily upon illustrations drawn from Linnaean Botany. But while the philosopher's exploitation of science is now likely to meet with severe criticism, we are perhaps too ready to accept the conclusions of the scientist when he philosophizes.

One effect of this striving of philosophy towards the condition of the exact sciences was that it produced the illusion of a progress of philosophy, of a kind to which philosophy should not pretend. It turned out philosophical pedagogues ignorant, not merely of history in the general sense, but of the history of philosophy itself. If our attitude towards philosophy is influenced by an admiration for the exact sciences, then the philosophy of the past is something that has been superseded. It is punctuated by individual philosophers, some of whom had moments of understanding, but whose work as a whole comes to be regarded as quaint and primitive. For the philosophy of the present, from this point of view, is altogether better than that of the past, when science was in its infancy; and the philosophy of the future will proceed from the discoveries of our own age. It is true that the history of philosophy is now admitted as a branch of study in itself, and that there are specialists in this subject: but I suspect that in the opinion of a philosopher of the modern school, the historian of philosophy is rather an historian than a philosopher.

The root cause of the vagaries of modern philosophy – and perhaps, though I was unconscious of it, the reason for my dissatisfaction with philosophy as a *profession* – I now believe to lie in the divorce of philosophy from theology. It is very necessary to anticipate the resistance to such an affirmation: a resistance springing from an immediate emotional response, and expressed by saying that any dependence of philosophy upon theology would be a limitation of the freedom of thought of the philosopher. It is necessary to make clear what one means by the necessary relation between philosophy and theology, and the implication in philosophy of some religious faith. This I shall not attempt, because it is done very much better by Josef Pieper: I desire only to call attention to this central point in his thought. He is himself a Catholic philosopher, grounded on Plato, Aristotle and the scholastics: and he makes his position quite clear to his readers. But his writings do not constitute a Christian *apologetic* – that, in his view, is a task for the theologian. For him, a philosophy related to the theology of some other communion than that of Rome, or to that of some other religion than Christianity, would still be a genuine philosophy. It is significant that he pays a passing word of approval to the existentialism of Sartre, on the ground that he finds in it religious presuppositions – utterly different as they are from those which Dr. Pieper holds himself.

The establishment of a right relation between philosophy and theology, which will leave the philosopher quite autonomous in his own area, is I think one of the most important lines of investigation which Dr. Pieper has pursued. In a more general way, his influence should be in the direction of restoring philosophy to a place of importance for every educated person who thinks, instead of confining it to esoteric activities which can affect the public only indirectly, insidiously and often in a distorted form. He restores to their position in philosophy what common sense obstinately tells us ought to be found there: *insight* and *wisdom*. By affirming the dependence of philosophy upon revelation, and a proper respect for 'the wisdom of the ancients', he puts the philosopher himself in a proper relation to other philosophers dead and living. Two dangers to philosophy are thus averted. One is the conscious or unconscious imitation of exact science, the assumption that philosophers should be organized as teams of workers, like scientists in their laboratories, investigating various parts of a problem which is conceived as soluble in the same way as a problem in physics. The opposite error is that of an older and more romantic attitude, which produced what I may call the 'one-man' philosophy: that is to say, a world view which was a projection of the personality of its author, a disguised imposition of his own temperament with all its emotional bias, upon the reader. I do not wish to diminish the grandeur or the value of the greatest one-man philosophies. When such a philosophy is done superbly well, as by Spinoza, it retains a permanent importance for humanity: for an acquaintance with Spinoza, and a temporary submission to his influence,

16

is an experience of great value. On the other hand, the colossal and grotesque achievement of Hegel may continue in concealed or derivative forms to exercise a fascination upon many minds. I would mention also the work of such a writer as F. H. Bradley, which owes its persuasiveness to a masterly prose style. The charm of the author's personality stimulates an agreeable state of feeling: and such books will continue to be read as literature, for the enlargement of our experience through a contact with powerful and individual minds.

Dr. Pieper also has style: however difficult his thought may sometimes be, his sentences are admirably constructed, his ideas expressed with the maximum clarity. But his mind is submissive to what he believes to be the great, the main tradition of European thought; his originality is subdued and unostentatious. And as he is a philosopher who accepts explicitly a dogmatic theology, his presuppositions are in full view, instead of being, as with some philosophers who profess complete detachment, concealed from both author and reader. The attitude towards philosophy which he maintains, and which distinguishes him from most of our contemporaries, is enough to account for his preference for expression in brief and concentrated essays rather than in constructions of greater bulk. Of such essays he has already published an impressive list: the two here presented are those which author, translator and publishers agreed upon as the most suitable introduction to his thought.   T. S. ELIOT

AUTHOR'S PREFACE
TO THE ENGLISH EDITION

These two essays were published separately in Germany, the second having been originally written in the form of lectures, given in Bonn in the summer of 1947. They are intimately connected and properly belong together. This is not only true in the sense that they were both written in the same summer, in a single breath, so to say; they both spring from the same thought.

Their common origin or foundation might be stated in the following words: Culture depends for its very existence on leisure, and leisure, in its turn, is not possible unless it has a durable and consequently living link with the *cultus*, with divine worship.

The word 'cult' in English is used exclusively, or almost exclusively, in a derivative sense. But here it is used, along with worship, in its primary sense. It means something else than, and something more than, religion. It really means fulfilling the ritual of public sacrifice. That is a notion which contemporary 'modern' man associates almost exclusively and unconsciously with uncivilized, primitive peoples and with classical antiquity. For that very reason it is of the first importance to see that the *cultus*, now as in the distant past, is the primary source of man's freedom, independence and immunity within society. Suppress that last sphere of freedom, and freedom itself, and all our liberties, will in the end vanish into thin air.

Culture, in the sense in which it is used above, is the quintessence of all the natural goods of the world and of those gifts and qualities which, while belonging to man, lie beyond the immediate sphere of his needs and wants. All that is good in this sense, all man's gifts and faculties are not necessarily useful in a practical way; though there is no denying that they belong to a truly human life, not strictly speaking necessary, even though he could not do without them.

Among the *bona non utilia sed honesta* which are at home in the realm of freedom, in its innermost circle indeed, is philosophy, the philosophical act, which must be understood in the traditional sense of Plato, Aristotle, Augustine and Aquinas, and as they understood it. Grant this original sense of the word 'philosophizing' to be the true one, and it is no longer possible to speak of the philosophical aspect in the same way that one might speak of a sociological and historical or a political aspect—as though one could take up the one or the other at will. In the tradition of which I am speaking, the philosophical act is a fundamental relation to reality, a full, personal attitude which is by no manner of means at the sole disposal of the *ratio*; it is an attitude which presupposes silence, a contem-

plative attention to things, in which man begins to
see how worthy of veneration they really are. And it
is perhaps only in this way that it is possible to understand how it was that Plato's philosophical school, the
Academy in Athens, was at the same time a sort of
club or society for the celebration of the *cultus*. In the
last resort pure theory, philosophical *theoria*, entirely
free from practical considerations and interference –
and that is what theory is – can only be preserved and
realized within the sphere of leisure, and leisure, in its
turn, is free because of its relation to worship, to the
cultus.

LEISURE
THE BASIS OF CULTURE

But the Gods, taking pity on mankind, born to work, laid down the succession of recurring Feasts to restore them from their fatigue, and gave them the Muses, and Apollo their leader, and Dionysus, as companions in their Feasts, so that nourishing themselves in festive companionship with the Gods, they should again stand upright and erect.

PLATO

Have leisure and know that I am God.

Psalm lxv, 11.

I

Let me begin with an objection, an objection of the kind which the scholastics called a *Videtur quod non*. Now of all times, in the post-war years is not the time to talk about leisure. We are, after all, busy building our house. Our hands are full and there is work for all. And surely, until our task is done and our house is rebuilt, the only thing that matters is to strain every nerve.

That is not an objection to be put lightly aside. And yet, whenever our task carries us beyond the maintenance of a bare existence and the satisfaction of our most pressing needs, once we are faced with reorganizing our intellectual and moral and spiritual assets—then, before discussing the problem in detail, a fresh start and new foundations call for a defence of leisure.

For assuming all too rashly, for the moment, that our new house is going to be built in the Western tradition—a thing so arguable that it might almost be said to be the decision which is hanging in the balance—it is essential to begin by reckoning with the fact that one of the foundations of Western culture is leisure. That much, at least, can be learnt from the first chapter of Aristotle's *Metaphysics*. And even the history of the word attests the fact: for leisure in Greek is *skole*, and in Latin *scola*, the English 'school'. The word used to designate the place where we educate and teach is derived from a word which means 'leisure'. 'School' does not, properly speaking, mean school, but leisure.

The original conception of leisure, as it arose in the civilized world of Greece, has, however, become unrecognizable in the world of planned diligence and 'total labour'; and in order to gain a clear notion of leisure we must begin by setting aside the prejudice —our prejudice—that comes from overvaluing the sphere of work. In his well-known study of capitalism Max Weber[1] quotes the saying, that 'one does not work to live; one lives to work', which nowadays no one has much difficulty in understanding: it expresses the current opinion. We even find some difficulty in grasping that it reverses the order of things and stands them on their head.

But what ought we to say to the opposite view, to the view that 'we work in order to have leisure'? We should not hesitate to say that here indeed 'the world of topsy-turvydom', the world that had been stood on its head, has been clearly expressed. To those who live in a world of nothing but work, in what we might call the world of 'total work', it presumably sounds immoral, as though directed at the very foundations of human society.

That maxim is not, however, an illustration invented for the sake of clarifying this thesis: it is a quotation from Aristotle; and the fact that it expresses the view of a cool-headed workaday realist (as he is supposed to have been) gives it all the more weight. Literally, the Greek says 'we are unleisurely in order to have leisure.'[2] 'To be unleisurely'—that is the word the Greeks used not only for the daily toil and moil of life, but for ordinary everyday work. Greek only has the negative, *a-scolia*, just as Latin has *neg-otium*.

The context of Aristotle's words, and his other statement (in the *Politics*) to the effect that leisure is the centre-point about which everything revolves,[3] seems to indicate that he was saying something almost self-evident; and one can only suppose that the Greeks would not have understood our maxims about 'work for work's sake' at all. On the other hand it must be evident that we no longer understand their conception of leisure simply and directly.

This is perhaps the point at which to anticipate the objection: 'What does Aristotle honestly matter to us? We may admire the world of antiquity, but why should we feel under any obligation to it?'

Among other things, it might be pointed out in reply that the Christian and Western conception of the contemplative life is closely linked to the Aristotelian notion of leisure. It is also to be observed that this is the source of the distinction between the *artes liberales* and the *artes serviles*, the liberal arts and servile work. And to the further objection that this distinction only interests historians, one might reply that everyone is familiar with at any rate one half of the distinction, from the fact that we still speak of 'servile work' as unsuitable on Sundays and holidays. Though who nowadays stops to think that 'servile work' and 'liberal arts' are twin expressions, and form, one might almost say, the articulation of a joint, so that the one is hardly intelligible without the other? For it is barely possible to think of 'servile work' with any degree of accuracy without delimiting the sense with reference to the 'liberal arts'.

All this, and much besides, might be adduced to show that Aristotle is more than a name; though it is true that purely historical considerations are no basis for an obligation.

But the immediate purpose was really to make it plain that the value we set on work and on leisure is very far from being the same as that of the Greek and Roman world, or of the Middle Ages, for that matter —so very different that the men of the past would have been incapable of understanding the modern conception of work, just as we are unable to understand their notion of leisure simply and directly, without an effort of thought. The tremendous difference of point of view implied and our relative ignorance of the notion of leisure emerge more clearly if we examine the notion of work in its modern form, spreading, as it does, to cover and include the whole of human activity

and even of human life; for then we shall realize to
what an extent we tacitly acknowledge the claims that
are made in the name of the 'worker'.

Here and in all that follows 'worker' must not be
taken as defining an occupation, as in statistical
works; it is *not* synonymous with 'proletarian'—
although the fact that the words are interchangeable
is significant. On the contrary, 'worker' will be used
in an anthropological sense; it implies a whole conception of 'man'. Ernst Niekisch was using the word
'worker' in this sense when he spoke of the 'worker'
as an 'imperial figure';[4] and Ernst Jünger[5] uses the
same term to outline the ideal image that, according
to him, has already begun to mould the man of the
future.

A new and changing conception of the nature of
man, a new and changing conception of the very
meaning of human existence—that is what comes to
light in the claims expressed in the modern notion
of 'work' and 'worker'. These great subterranean
changes in our scale of values, and in the meaning of
value, are never easy to detect and lay bare, and they
can certainly not be seen at a glance. And if we are
to succeed in our purpose and uncover this great
change, an historical treatment of the subject will be
altogether inadequate; it becomes necessary to dig
down to the roots of the problem and so base our
conclusions on a philosophical and theological conception of man.

II

'Intellectual work' and 'intellectual worker' are the signposts indicating the last stretch of the historical journey, an historical journey in the course of which the modern ideal of work was defined in its final and extreme form—for the terms are relatively modern.

Intellectual activity used always to be considered a privileged sphere, and from the standpoint of the manual worker specially, appeared to be a sphere in which one did not need to work. Within that sphere, the province of philosophy and of philosophical culture seemed furthest from the world of work. But nowadays the whole field of intellectual activity, not excepting the province of philosophical culture, has been overwhelmed by the modern ideal of work and is at the mercy of its totalitarian claims. That is the latest phase of the struggle for power, of the process whereby that 'imperial figure' the 'worker' seizes power. And the seizure of power is revealed in the conceptions 'intellectual work' and 'intellectual worker' and in the claims, too, which they imply.

The last stretch of the road has one advantage from the point of the spectator: it sums up the whole historical movement once again in a single formula of the utmost concision and clarity. The real meaning of the ideal of the world of 'total work' reveals itself if one examines the inner structure of the concept 'intellectual work' and follows it down to its ultimate conclusions.

The concept 'intellectual worker' may be analysed from any one of its several sources in history. It implies, in the first place, a very definite view of the mode and manner of man's intellectual knowledge. What happens when we look at a rose? What do we do as we become aware of colour and form? Our soul is passive and receptive. We are, to be sure, awake and active, but our attention is not strained; we simply 'look'—in so far, that is, as we 'contemplate' it and are not already 'observing' it (for 'observing' implies that we are beginning to count, to measure and to weigh up). Observation is a tense activity; which is what Ernst Jünger meant when he called seeing an 'act of aggression'.[1] To contemplate, on the other hand, to 'look' in this sense, means to open one's eyes receptively to whatever offers itself to one's vision, and the things seen enter into us, so to speak, without calling for any effort or strain on our part to possess them. There can hardly be any doubt that that, or something like it, is the way we become sensorially aware of a thing.

But what of knowledge, the mind's spiritual knowledge? Is there such a thing as a purely receptive attitude of mind in which we become aware of immaterial

31

reality and invisible relationships? Is there such a thing as pure 'intellectual contemplation'—to adopt the terminology of the schools? In antiquity the answer given was always yes; in modern philosophy, for the most part, the answer given is no.

Kant, for example, held knowledge to be exclusively 'discursive': that is to say, the opposite of receptive and contemplative; and his opinion on this point has quite recently been called 'the most momentous dogmatic assumption of Kantian epistemology'.[2] According to Kant man's knowledge is realized in the act of comparing, examining, relating, distinguishing, abstracting, deducing, demonstrating—all of which are forms of active intellectual effort. Knowledge, man's spiritual, intellectual knowledge (such is Kant's thesis) is activity, exclusively activity.

Working on that basis, Kant was bound to reach the view that knowing and philosophizing (philosophizing in particular, since it is furthest removed from purely physical awareness) must be regarded and understood as *work*. And lest there should be any doubt on the point he said so explicitly in an article written, in 1796, against the romantic, contemplative and intuitive philosophy of Jacobi, Schlosser and Stolberg.[3] In philosophy, we read there, 'the law is that reason acquires its possessions through work.' The philosophy of the romantics is not genuine philosophy because it involves no work—a reproach that could, in some measure, be levelled at Plato himself,

32

'the father of enthusiasm in philosophy'; 'whereas,' he continues, with reverent agreement, 'the philosophy of Aristotle is work.' Opinions, he says, such as those of the romantics, the sense that philosophy was above 'work', have been responsible for 'the new, superior tone in philosophy': a pseudo-philosophy 'in which there is no need to work; one only has to attend to the oracle in one's breast and enjoy it, and so possess that wisdom whole and entire, which is the end of philosophy'—a pseudo-philosophy that thinks it can look down haughtily on the effort and work of the true philosopher. So much for Immanuel Kant.

The philosophers of antiquity thought otherwise on this matter—though of course their view is very far from offering grounds of justification for those who take the easy path. The Greeks—Aristotle no less than Plato—as well as the great medieval thinkers, held that not only physical, sensuous perception, but equally man's spiritual and intellectual knowledge, included an element of pure, receptive contemplation, or as Heraclitus says, of 'listening to the essence of things'.[4]

The Middle Ages drew a distinction between the understanding as *ratio* and the understanding as *intellectus*. *Ratio* is the power of discursive, logical thought, of searching and of examination, of abstraction, of definition and drawing conclusions. *Intellectus*, on the other hand, is the name for the understanding in so far as it is the capacity of *simplex intuitus*, of that simple vision to which truth offers itself like a landscape to the eye. The faculty of mind, man's knowledge, is both these things in one, according to antiquity and the Middle Ages, simultaneously *ratio* and *intellectus*; and the process of knowing is the action of the two together. The mode of discursive thought is accompanied and impregnated by an effortless awareness, the contemplative vision of the *intellectus*, which is not active but passive, or rather receptive, the activity of the soul in which it conceives that which it sees.

It should, however, be added that even the philosophers of antiquity (which here and elsewhere always means the philosophers of Greece and the Middle Ages) looked upon the active effort of discursive thought as the properly human element in our knowledge; it is the *ratio*, they held, which is distinctively human; the *intellectus* they regarded as being already beyond the sphere allotted to man. And yet it belonged to man, though in one sense 'superhuman'; the 'purely human' by itself could not satiate man's powers of comprehension, for man, of his very nature, reaches out beyond the sphere of the 'human', touching on the order of pure spirits. 'Although the knowledge which is most characteristic of the human soul occurs in the mode of *ratio*, nevertheless there is in it a sort of participation in the simple knowledge which is proper to higher beings, of whom it is therefore said that they possess the faculty of spiritual vision.' That is how the matter is put by Aquinas in the *Quaestiones disputate de veritate*.[5] It means to say that man participates in the angelic faculty of non-discursive vision, which is the capacity to apprehend the spiritual in the same manner that our eye apprehends light or our ear sound. Our knowledge in fact includes an element of non-activity, of purely receptive vision—though it is certainly not essentially human; it is, rather, the fulfilment of the highest promise in man, and thus, again, truly human (just as Aquinas calls the *vita contemplativa* 'non proprie humana sed superhumana',[6] not really human but superhuman, although it is the noblest way of life).

The philosophical tradition of antiquity did, therefore, recognize the element of work in man's mode of knowledge as specifically human. For the use of the *ratio*, discursive thought, requires real hard work.

The simple vision of the *intellectus*, however, contemplation, is *not* work. If, as this philosophical tradition holds, man's spiritual knowledge is the fruit of *ratio* and *intellectus*; if the discursive element is fused with 'intellectual contemplation' and if, moreover, knowledge in philosophy, which is directed upon the whole of being, is to preserve the element of contemplation, then it is not enough to describe this knowledge as work, for that would be to omit something essential. Knowledge in general, and more especially philosophical knowledge, is certainly quite impossible without work, without the *labor improbus* of discursive thought. Nevertheless there is also that about it which, essentially, is not work.

The statement that 'knowledge is work'—because 'knowing' is activity, pure activity—has two aspects: it expresses a claim *on* man and a claim *by* man. If you want to know something then you must work; in philosophy 'the law is that reason acquires its possessions through work'[7] that is the claim on man. But there is another, a subtler claim, not perhaps immediately visible, in the statement, the claim made by man: if to know is to work, then knowledge is the fruit of our own unaided effort and activity; then knowledge includes nothing which is not due to the effort of man, and there is nothing *gratuitous* about it, nothing 'in-spired', nothing 'given' about it.

To sum up: the essence of human cognition, on this view, is that it is exclusively an active, discursive labour of the *ratio*, the reason; and the notion 'intellectual work' and 'intellectual worker' acquires a quite special weight if we accept this point of view.

Look at the 'worker' and you will see that his face is marked by strain and tension, and these are even more pronounced in the case of the 'intellectual worker'. These are the marks of that perpetual activity (exclusive of all else) of which Goethe remarked that 'it ends in bankruptcy'.[8] They are the revealing marks of the intellectual sclerosis that comes with not being able to receive or accept, of that hardening of the heart that refuses to suffer anything; and in their extreme form such tensions become vocal in the lunatic assertion 'every action has some meaning, even a crime; but to be passive is always senseless.'[9]

Now discursive thought and intellectual contemplation are not simply related to one another as activity to receptivity, or as tense effort to passive acceptance. They are also related to one another as toil and trouble on the one hand and effortless possession on the other. And this antithesis—toil and trouble on one side, effortless ease on the other—is the occasion of yet another reason for the special stress on the notion of 'intellectual work'. So that we must now consider, for a moment, a particular view of the criterion of the worth and worthlessness of human behaviour in general.

When Kant speaks of philosophizing as a 'herculean labour',[10] he does not simply mean that it is characteristic of philosophizing; he regards the labour involved as a justification of philosophy: philosophizing is genuine in so far as it is 'herculean labour'. And it is because, as he contemptuously remarks, 'intellectual contemplation' costs nobody anything that it is so very questionable. He expects nothing from 'intellectual contemplation' *because* it costs nothing, and because contemplation is effortless. But that is surely on the way (if not even closer) to the view that the *effort* of acquiring knowledge gives one the assurance of the material *truth* of the knowledge acquired.

And there, in turn, we are not so very far from the

37

ethical notion that everything man does naturally and without effort is a falsification of true morality—for what we do by nature is done without effort. In Kant's view, indeed, the fact that man's natural bent is contrary to the moral law, belongs to the concept of moral law. It is normal and essential, on this view, that the good should be difficult, and that the effort of will required in forcing oneself to perform some action should become the yardstick of the moral good: the more difficult a thing, the higher it is in the order of goodness. Schiller's ironical couplet hits off the weakness of this point of view:

> *Gerne dient'ich den Freunden, doch tu ich es leider*
> *mit Neigung,*
> *Und so wurmt es mir oft, dass ich nicht tugendhaft*
> *bin.*[11]
> *(How willingly I'd serve my friends, but alas, I do*
> *so with pleasure,*
> *And so I am often worried by the fact that I am not*
> *virtuous.)*

Hard work, then, is what is good. That is not by any means a new view, and it was put forward by Antisthenes the Cynic,[12] one of Plato's companions among those who grouped themselves round Socrates. Antisthenes is one of those surprisingly modern figures that occur here and there, and it is he who left us the first sketch of the 'worker', or more accurately, perhaps, who represents that figure. Antisthenes is not only the author of the phrase just quoted about hard work; he is also responsible for making Hercules the human ideal, because he performed superhuman labours[13]: an ideal that has retained (or has it re-acquired it?) a certain force from the days of Erasmus[14] and Kant—who labelled philosophy with the heroic term 'herculean'—down to those of Carlyle, the prophet of the religion of work[15]: You must work like Hercules. . . . Antisthenes the Cynic was a self-sufficient moralist, an autarchist, with no sense whatsoever of divine worship, even cracking Voltairian jokes about it[16]; he was insensible to the Muses and only liked poetry when it served to express moral truths[17]; and as for Eros, it evoked no reply in his heart: 'Best of all,' he remarked, 'I would like to exterminate Aphrodite.'[18] A dry realist, he did not, of course, believe in immortality; the one thing that matters is to live 'an upright life' in this world.[19] It really looks as though all these traits had been gathered into one for the sake of providing an example in the abstract of the type 'worker' pure and undefiled.

'Hard work is what is good'—but in the *Summa Theologica* we find St. Thomas maintaining the diametrically opposite opinion: 'The essence of virtue consists in the good rather than in the difficult.'[20] 'Not everything that is more difficult is necessarily more meritorious; it must be more difficult in such a way that it is at the same time good in a yet higher way.'[21] The Middle Ages also said something about virtue that is no longer so readily understood—least of all by Kant's compatriots and disciples—they held that virtue meant: 'mastering our natural bent'. No; that is what Kant would have said, and we all of us find it quite easy to understand; what Aquinas says is that virtue makes us perfect by enabling us to *follow* our natural bent in the right way.[22] The highest moral good is characterized by effortlessness—because it springs from love.

The tendency to overvalue hard work and the effort of doing something *difficult* is so deep-rooted that it even infects our notion of love. Why should it be that the average Christian regards loving one's enemy as the most exalted form of love? Principally because it offers an example of a natural bent heroically curbed; the exceptional difficulty, the impossibility one might almost say, of loving one's enemy constitutes the greatness of the love. And what does Aquinas say? 'It is not the difficulty of loving one's enemy that matters when the essence of the merit of doing so is concerned, excepting in so far as the perfection of love wipes out the difficulty. And therefore, if love were to be so perfect that the difficulty vanished altogether —it would be more meritorious still.'[23]

And in the same way, the essence of thought does not consist in the effort for which it calls, but in grasping existing things and in unveiling reality. Moreover, just as the highest form of virtue knows nothing of 'difficulty', so too the highest form of

40

knowledge comes to man like a gift—the sudden illumination, a stroke of genius, true contemplation; it comes effortlessly and without trouble. On one occasion St. Thomas speaks of contemplation and play in the same breath: 'because of the leisure that goes with contemplation' the divine wisdom itself, Holy Scripture says, is 'always at play, playing through the whole world' (Proverbs viii, 30 f.).[24]

The highest forms of knowledge, on the other hand, may well be preceded by a great effort of thought, and perhaps this must be so (unless the knowledge in question were grace in the strict sense of the word); but in any case, the effort is not the cause; it is the condition. It is equally true that the effects so effortlessly produced by love presuppose no doubt an heroic moral struggle of the will. But the decisive thing is that virtue means the realization of the good; it may imply a previous moral effort, but it cannot be equated with moral effort. And similarly, to know means to reach the reality of existing things; knowledge is not confined to effort of thought. It is more than 'intellectual work'.

This aspect too of 'intellectual work'—the exaggerated value which is put upon the 'difficult' simply because it is difficult—becomes evident in the accentuation of a particular trait in the look of the 'worker': the fixed, mask-like readiness to suffer *in vacuo*, without relation to anything. It is the absence of any connection with reality or real values that is distinctive. And it is because this readiness to suffer (which

41

has been called the heart of discipline, of whatever kind)[25] never asks the question 'to what end' that it is utterly different from the Christian conception of sacrifice. The Christian conception of sacrifice is not concerned with the suffering involved *qua* suffering, it is not primarily concerned with the toil and the worry and with the difficulty, but with salvation, with the fullness of being, and thus ultimately with the fullness of happiness: 'The end and the norm of discipline is happiness'.[26]

The inmost significance of the exaggerated value which is set upon hard work appears to be this: man seems to mistrust everything that is effortless; he can only enjoy, with a good conscience, what he has acquired with toil and trouble; he refuses to have anything as a gift.

We have only to think for a moment how much of the Christian understanding of life depends upon belief in Grace; to think that the Holy Spirit is in a special sense a 'gift'[27]; to think that the doctors of the Church hold that God's justice follows from his love[28]; that everything gained and everything claimed follows upon something given, and comes after something gratuitous and unearned; that in the beginning there is always a gift—we have only to think of all this for a moment in order to see what a chasm separates the tradition of the Christian West and that other view.

In attempting to get to the source of the notion

'intellectual work', we have seen that it can be traced in the main to two principal themes: the first is the view which regards human knowledge as exclusively attributable to discursive thought; the second is the contention that the effort which knowledge requires is a criterion of its truth. There is, however, a third element, more important than either of the foregoing, and which appears to involve both of them. It is the social implication of 'intellectual work' that comes more fully to light in the expression 'intellectual worker'.

Work as it is understood in this phrase and context means the same thing as social service. 'Intellectual work' in this context would mean intellectual activity in so far as it is a social service, in so far as it is a contribution to the common need. But that is not all that is implied by the words 'intellectual work' and 'intellectual worker'. In the current usage of today what is further implied is respect for the 'working class'. What is really meant is roughly this: like the wage-earner, the manual-worker and the proletarian, the educated man, the scholar, too, is a worker, in fact an 'intellectual worker', and he, too, is harnessed to the social system and takes his place in the division of labour; he is allotted his place and his function among the workers; he is a functionary in the world of 'total work'; he may be called a specialist, but he is a functionary. And that is what brings out the problem which really lies behind our question, in all its colours.

43

That problem, it need hardly be said, is not just a theoretical one; it is the root problem with which we began our discussion: are we to build our house in the European tradition?

And yet the social aspect, as it concerns the relations of the strata of society and of its various groups, is only the foreground of the question; and to that we shall return. The real question is a metaphysical one. It is the old question of the rights and the meaning of the liberal arts. What are the liberal arts? In his commentary on Aristotle's *Metaphysics*, Aquinas gives this definition: 'Only those arts are called liberal or free which are concerned with knowledge; those which are concerned with utilitarian ends that are attained through activity, however, are called servile.'[29] 'I know well,' Newman says, 'that knowledge may resolve itself into an art, and seminate in a mechanical process and in tangible fruit; but it may also fall back upon that Reason, which informs it, and resolve itself into Philosophy. For in one case it is called Useful Knowledge, in the other Liberal.'[30] The liberal arts, then, include all forms of human activity which are an end in themselves; the servile arts are those which have an end beyond themselves, and more precisely an end which consists in a utilitarian result attainable in practice, a practicable result.

Put in this form the question will seem to many people an anachronism, and the very terms 'liberal arts' and 'servile arts' sound antiquated and meaningless. But translated into the terminology of the present day the question means precisely this: Is there a sphere of human activity, one might even say of human existence, that does not need to be justified by inclusion in a five-year plan and its technical organization? Is there such a thing, or not? The inner meaning of the concepts 'intellectual work' and 'intellectual worker' points to the answer 'No'. Man, from this point of view, is essentially a functionary, an official, even in the highest reaches of his activity.

Let us consider the question from the point of view of philosophical education, which is the extreme case, and perhaps even the test case, of the liberal arts.* What does Newman say? 'Knowledge is then most truly free when it is philosophical knowledge.'[31] The rights of education itself are here at stake—education as opposed to training, culture as opposed to instruction—in so far as it is something more and something other than training for a profession, or trade. A functionary is trained. Training is defined as being concerned with some one side or aspect of man, with regard to some special subject. Education concerns the whole man; an educated man is a man with a point of view from which he takes in the whole world. Education concerns the whole man, man *capax universi*, capable of grasping the totality of existing things.

This implies nothing against training and nothing

* This question is treated at greater length on pp. 103 ff.

against the official. Of course specialized and professional work is *normal, the* normal way in which men play their part in the world; 'work' is the normal, the working day is the ordinary day. But the question is: whether the world, defined as the world of work, is exhaustively defined; can man develop to the full as a functionary and a 'worker' and nothing else; can a full human existence be contained within an exclusively workaday existence? Stated differently and translated back into our terms: is there such a thing as a liberal art? The doctrinaire planners of the world of 'total work' must answer 'No'. The worker's world, as Ernst Jünger puts it, is 'the denial of free scholarship and enquiry'.[32] In a consistently planned 'worker' State there is no room for philosophy because philosophy cannot serve other ends than its own or it ceases to be philosophy; nor can the sciences be carried on in a philosophical manner, which means to say that there can be no such thing as university (academic) education in the full sense of the word. And it is above all the expression 'intellectual worker' that epigrammatically confirms the fact that this is impossible. And that is why it is so alarmingly symptomatic that ordinary usage, and even university custom, allows the term 'intellectual worker' and sometimes permits 'brain worker'.

In antiquity the place of the liberal arts was recognized; the non-useful too had its rights in human affairs. The knowledge of the functionary is not the

46

only knowledge; there is also 'the knowledge of a gentleman' (to use Newman's very happy formula in the Idea of a University, for the term *artes liberales*).

There is no need to waste words showing that not everything is useless which cannot be brought under the definition of the useful. And it is by no means unimportant for a nation and for the realization of the 'common good', that a place should be made for activity which is not 'useful work' in the sense of being utilitarian. 'I have never bothered or asked', Goethe said to Friedrich Soret in 1830, 'in what way I was useful to society as a whole; I contented myself with expressing what I recognized as good and true. That has certainly been useful in a wide circle; but that was not the aim; it was the necessary result.'[33]

In the Middle Ages the same view prevailed. 'It is necessary for the perfection of human society', Aquinas writes, 'that there should be men who devote their lives to contemplation'[34]—*nota bene*, necessary not only for the good of the individual who so devotes himself, but for the good of human society. No one thinking in terms of 'intellectual worker' could have said that.

Cf. Rousseau, First Discourse

III

The 'worker', it has been seen, in our brief analysis of that significant figure, is characterized by three principal traits: an extreme tension of the powers of action, a readiness to suffer *in vacuo* unrelated to anything, and complete absorption in the social organism, itself rationally planned to utilitarian ends. Leisure, from this point of view, appears as something wholly fortuitous and strange, without rhyme or reason, and, morally speaking, unseemly: another word for laziness, idleness and sloth. At the zenith of the Middle Ages, on the contrary, it was held that sloth and restlessness, 'leisurelessness', the incapacity to enjoy leisure, were all closely connected; sloth was held to be the source of restlessness, and the ultimate cause of 'work for work's sake'. It may well seem paradoxical to maintain that the restlessness at the bottom of a fanatical and suicidal activity should come from the lack of will to action; a surprising thought, that we shall only be able to decipher with effort. But it is a worth-while effort, and we should do well to pause for a moment to enquire into the philosophy of life attached to the word *acedia*.[1]

48

In the first place *acedia* does not signify the 'idleness' we envisage when we speak of idleness as 'the root of all vice'. Idleness, in the medieval view, means that a man prefers to forgo the rights, or if you prefer the claims, that belong to his nature. In a word, he does not want to be as God wants him to be, and that ultimately means that he does not wish to be what he really, fundamentally, *is*. *Acedia* is the 'despair from weakness' which Kierkegaard analysed as the 'despairing refusal to be oneself'.[2] Metaphysically and theologically, the notion of *acedia* means that a man does not, in the last resort, give the consent of his will to his own being; that behind or beneath the dynamic activity of his existence, he is still not at one with himself, or, as the medieval writers would have said, face to face with the divine good within him; he is a prey to sadness (and that sadness is the *tristitia saeculi* of Holy Scripture).[3]

And then we are told that the opposite of this metaphysical and theological notion is the notion 'hardworking', industrious, in the context of economic life! For *acedia* has, in fact, been interpreted as though it had something to do with the economic ethos of the Middle Ages. Sombart, for example, treats it as though it were the fault of the lazy stay-at-home as compared with the industrious worker[4]—though Max Scheler criticized his view.[5] And some of Sombart's successors even go so far as to translate *acedia* as 'stick-in-the-mud'—as well say 'lack of business enterprise' or

49

even 'lack of salesmanship'.[6] All this, however, is less painful than the eager attempt of the apologist to make Christian teaching square with a passing fashion, which in this case involves interpreting the Church's view of work in terms of modern activism— with the result that *vivere secundum actum est quando exercet quis opera vitae in actu*[7] is actually translated as 'life in actu consists in this, that one is busy and occupied with practical affairs'[8] . . . as if Aquinas did not hold that contemplation was an *opus vitae*!

No, the contrary of *acedia* is not the spirit of work in the sense of the work of every day, of earning one's living; it is man's happy and cheerful affirmation of his own being, his acquiescence in the world and in God —which is to say love. Love that certainly brings a particular freshness and readiness to work along with it, but that no one with the least experience could conceivably confuse with the tense activity of the fanatical 'worker'.

Who would guess, unless he were expressly told so, that Aquinas regarded *acedia* as a sin against the third commandment? He was in fact so far from considering idleness as the opposite of the ethos of work that he simply interprets it as an offence against the commandment in which we are called upon to have 'the peace of the mind in God'.[9]

But what has all this, one might well ask, to do with the question? *Acedia* was reckoned among the *vitia capitalia*, as one of the seven capital or cardinal sins, for they were not called 'capital' because of the best-known rendering of *caput*; *caput* certainly means 'head', but it also means 'source' or 'spring'—and that is the meaning in this case. They are sins from which other faults follow 'naturally', one is tempted to say, as from a source. Idleness—and this is how we get back to the question—idleness, according to traditional teaching, is the source of many faults and among others of that deep-seated lack of calm which makes leisure impossible. Among other faults, certainly, and one of the children of *acedia*, is despair, which amounts to saying that despair and the incapacity for leisure are twins—a revealing thought that ex plains, among other things, the hidden meaning of that very questionable saying, 'work and don't despair'.

Idleness, in the old sense of the word, so far from being synonymous with leisure, is more nearly the inner prerequisite which renders leisure impossible: it might be described as the utter absence of leisure, or the very opposite of leisure. Leisure is only possible when a man is at one with himself, when he acquiesces in his own being, whereas the essence of *acedia* is the refusal to acquiesce in one's own being. Idleness and the incapacity for leisure correspond with one another. Leisure is the contrary of both.

Leisure, it must be clearly understood, is a mental and spiritual attitude—it is not simply the result of external factors, it is not the inevitable result of spare time, a holiday, a week-end or a vacation. It is, in the first place, an attitude of mind, a condition of the soul, and as such utterly contrary to the ideal of 'worker' in each and every one of the three aspects under which it was analysed: work as activity, as toil, as a social function.

Compared with the exclusive ideal of work as activity, leisure implies (in the first place) an attitude of non-activity, of inward calm, of silence; it means not being 'busy', but letting things happen.

Leisure is a form of silence, of that silence which is the prerequisite of the apprehension of reality: only the silent hear and those who do not remain silent do not hear. Silence, as it is used in this context, does not mean 'dumbness' or 'noiselessness'; it means more nearly that the soul's power to 'answer' to the reality of the world is left undisturbed. For leisure is a receptive attitude of mind, a contemplative attitude, and it is not only the occasion but also the capacity for steeping oneself in the whole of creation.

Furthermore there is also a certain happiness in leisure, something of the happiness that comes from the recognition of the mysteriousness of the universe and the recognition of our incapacity to understand it, that comes with a deep confidence, so that we are content to let things take their course; and there is something about it which Konrad Weiss, the poet, called 'confidence in the fragmentariness of life and history'. In the same entry in his Journal he refers to the characteristically precise style and thought of Ernst Jünger, with his fanaticism for the truth[10]— Jünger, who really seems to tear the mystery out of a thing, coldly and boldly, and then lay it out, neatly dissected, all ready to view. His passion for tidy formulae 'is surely the very reverse of contemplative, and yet there is something idle in it, idleness concealed within the sublime exactitude of thought—as opposed to the true idleness which lets God and the world and things go, and gives them time . . .'!

Leisure is not the attitude of mind of those who actively intervene, but of those who are open to everything; not of those who grab and grab hold, but of those who leave the reins loose and who are free and easy themselves—almost like a man falling asleep, for one can only fall asleep by 'letting oneself go'. Sleeplessness and the incapacity for leisure are really related to one another in a special sense, and a man at leisure is not unlike a man asleep. Heraclitus the Obscure observed of men who were asleep that they too 'were busy and active in the happenings of the world'.[11] When we really let our minds rest contemplatively on a rose in bud, on a child at play, on a divine mystery, we are rested and quickened as though by a dreamless sleep. Or as the Book of Job says 'God giveth songs in the night' (Job xxxv, 10). Moreover, it has always been a pious belief that God sends his good gifts and his blessings in sleep. And in the same way his great, imperishable intuitions visit a man in his moments of leisure. It is in these silent and receptive moments that the soul of man is sometimes visited by an awareness of what holds the world together:

was die Welt
Im innersten zusammenhält

only for a moment perhaps, and the lightning vision of his intuition has to be recaptured and rediscovered in hard work.

Compared with the exclusive ideal of work as toil, leisure appears (*secondly*) in its character as an attitude of contemplative 'celebration', a word that, properly understood, goes to the very heart of the meaning which I am concerned to put before you. Leisure is only possible, to recall what has already been said, to a man at one with himself, but who is also at one with the world. Those are the 'presuppositions' of leisure, for leisure is an affirmation. Idleness, on the contrary, is rooted in the omission of those two affirmations.

Leisure, it may be re-stated, is not just non-activity, it is not the same as quiet and peace, not even inward quiet and peace, though there is a silence in the dialogue of love to which it might be compared. Something of this is conveyed in Hölderlin's fragment *Leisure*, where he compares himself to a loving elm standing in a peaceful meadow, while the delight of life plays about him, embracing him like a vine:

> *ich stehe im friedlichen Felde*
> *Wie ein liebender Ulmbaum da, und wie Reben und*
>   *Trauben*
> *Schlingen sich rund um mich die süssen Spiele des*
>   *Lebens.*

God, we are told in the first chapter of Genesis, 'ended his work which he had made' and 'behold, it was very good'. In the same way man celebrates and gratefully accepts the reality of creation in leisure, and the inner vision that accompanies it. And just as Holy Scripture tells us that God rested on the seventh day and beheld that 'the work which he had made' was 'very good'—so too it is leisure which leads man to accept the reality of the creation and thus to celebrate it, resting on the inner vision that accompanies it.

The strongest affirmation of this agreement is the celebration of a feast, where 'to celebrate', as Karl Kerényi says, is 'the union of peace, contemplation and intensity of life'.[12] In all religions, the meaning of a feast has always been the same, the affirmation of man's fundamental accord with the world; and its purpose is to express this accord and man's participation in the world in a special manner. Feast days and holy-days are the inner source of leisure. It is because leisure takes its origin from 'celebration' that it is not only effortless but the direct contrary of effort; not just the negative, in the sense of being no effort, but the positive counterpart.

And *thirdly*, leisure stands opposed to the exclusive ideal of work *qua* social function. A break in one's work, whether of an hour, a day or a week, is still part of the world of work. It is a link in the chain of utilitarian functions. The pause is made for the sake of work and in order to work, and a man is not only refreshed *from* work but *for* work. Leisure is an altogether different matter; it is no longer on the same plane; it runs at right angles to work—just as it could be said that intuition is not the prolongation or continuation, as it were, of the work of the *ratio*, but cuts right across it, vertically. *Ratio*, in point of fact, used to be compared to time, whereas *intellectus* was compared to eternity, to the eternal now.[13] And therefore leisure does not exist for the sake of work—however much strength it may give a man to work; the point of leisure is not to be a restorative, a pick-me-up, whether mental or physical; and though it gives new strength, mentally and physically, and spiritually too, that is not the point.

Leisure, like contemplation, is of a higher order than the *vita activa* (although the active life is the proper human life in a more special sense). And order, in this sense, cannot be overturned or reversed. Thus, however true it may be that the man who says his nightly prayers sleeps the better for it, nevertheless no one could say his nightly prayers with that in mind.

In the same way, no one who looks to leisure simply to restore his working powers will ever discover the fruit of leisure; he will never know the quickening that follows, almost as though from some deep sleep.

The point and the justification of leisure are not that the functionary should function faultlessly and without a breakdown, but that the functionary should continue to be a man—and that means that he should not be wholly absorbed in the clear-cut milieu of his strictly limited function; the point is also that he should continue to be capable of seeing life as a whole and the world as a whole; that he should fulfil himself, and come to full possession of his faculties, face to face with being as a whole.

That is the sense in which the powers necessary to enjoy leisure are among the fundamental powers of the human soul. Like the gift of contemplation in which the soul steeps itself in being, and the capacity to raise up the mind and heart and 'celebrate', in the full religious sense of the word, leisure is the power of stepping beyond the workaday world, and in so doing touching upon the superhuman life-giving powers which, incidentally almost, renew and quicken us for our everyday tasks. It is only in and through leisure that the 'gate to freedom' is opened and man can escape from the closed circle of that 'latent dread and anxiety' which a clear-sighted observer has perceived to be the mark of the world of work, where 'work and unemployment are the two inescapable poles of existence'.[14]

In leisure—not of course exclusively in leisure, but always in leisure—the truly human values are saved and preserved *because* leisure is the means whereby the sphere of the 'specifically human' can, over and again, be left behind—not as a result of any violent effort to escape, but as in an ecstasy (the ecstasy is indeed more 'difficult' than the most violent exertion, more 'difficult' because not invariably at our beck and call; a state of extreme tension is more easily induced than a state of relaxation and ease *although* the latter is effortless); the full enjoyment of leisure is hedged in by paradoxes of this kind, and it is itself a state at once very human and superhuman. Aristotle says of leisure, 'A man will live thus, not to the extent that he is a man, but to the extent that a divine principle dwells within him.'[15]

IV

In the foregoing sections leisure was tentatively defined and outlined in its ideal form. It now remains to consider the problem of realizing its 'hopes', of its latent powers of gaining acceptance, and its possible impetus in history. The practical problem involved might be stated thus: Is it possible, from now on, to maintain and defend, or even to reconquer, the right and claims of leisure, in face of the claims of 'total·labour' that are invading every sphere of life? Leisure, it must be remembered, is not a Sunday afternoon idyll, but the preserve of freedom, of education and culture, and of that undiminished humanity which views the world as a whole. In other words, is it going to be possible to save men from becoming officials and functionaries and 'workers' to the exclusion of all else? Can that possibly be done, and if so in what circumstances? There is no doubt of one thing: the world of the 'worker' is taking shape with dynamic force—with such a velocity that, rightly or wrongly, one is tempted to speak of daemonic force in history.

The attempt to withstand this invasion has been made at a number of different points for some time past. It is even possible to lay down that certain forms

of opposition are inadequate; for example the position
—quite legitimate up to a point—called 'art for art's
sake', was an attempt to isolate the realm of art from
the universal utilitarianism that seeks to turn everything in the world to some useful purpose. In our own
day, when the real historical fronts still remain to
some extent fluid, masked by provisional 'restora-
tions', the following defensive positions may be noted:
a renewed understanding of tradition in the widest
sense of the word; an emphasis on our duty as the
heirs of classical antiquity; the struggle to retain the
classics in the schools and the 'academic' (philosophical) character of the universities—in a word
humanism. Such are the designations of some of the
positions from which a threatened and endangered
body aspires to defend itself.

The question is whether these positions will be held
and in fact whether they *can* be held. The problem is
whether 'Humanism' is an adequate watchword—
adequate, not simply as a psychologically good rallying
cry, as an effective summons to battle, but as a
conception metaphysically sound and therefore ultimately credible, in the sense of providing a genuine
source of power capable of influencing the course of
history. ('Humanism', it should here be observed, has
recently made its appearance in Eastern Germany,
where it has become the fashion to speak of economic
materialism as 'humanistic'; and in France, an athe-
istic existentialism also claims to be humanistic—

neither usage, what is more, is entirely without justification!) The real question is therefore, whether an
appeal to 'humanism' is adequate—in face of the
totalitarian claims of the world of work.

Before attempting to answer the question there are
one or two misunderstandings already stirring that
need to be disposed of in an

Excursus on the meaning of 'proletariat'

It has already been explained that the term 'intellectual worker' adds pointed expression to the claims of
the world of work. But a modern German dictionary
(Trübner's) maintains, on the contrary, that the relatively modern terms 'intellectual work', 'intellectual
worker' are valuable because 'they do away with the
age-old distinction, still further emphasized in modern
times, between the manual worker and the educated
man'.[1] Now, if that designation is *not* accepted, or at
least only with reservations, it surely implies a certain
conception of those social contrasts? The refusal to
allow the validity of the term 'intellectual worker'
certainly means one thing: it means that the common
denominator 'work' and 'worker' is not considered a
proper or a possible basis upon which to bridge the
contrast of the classes of society. But does it not mean
something more? Does it not mean that the gulf between an educated class which is free to pursue
knowledge as an end in itself, and the proletarian
who knows nothing beyond the spare-time which is

61

barely sufficient for him to renew his strength for his daily work—does it not mean logically, from our point of view, that this gulf is in fact necessarily deepened and widened, independently of whatever subjective views and intentions may be at work? This objection is not to be taken lightly.

Indeed, on one occasion Plato contrasts the figure of the philosopher with that of the *bánausos*, the common working man. Philosophers are those 'who have not grown up like serfs, but in quite different, not to say contrary, circumstances. Now this, O Theodorus, is the way of each one individually: the one whom you call a philosopher, is truly brought up in freedom and leisure, and goes unpunished though he seems simple and useless when it is a matter of menial offices, even though he should not, for instance, know how to tie up a parcel that has to be sent on, or how to prepare a tasty dish . . .; the other way is the way of those who know, indeed, how to perform all these things well and smartly, but on the other hand do not even know how to wear their cloak like a gentleman, and still less how to prize the good life of gods and men in harmonious phrases.' This passage is to be found in Plato's *Theaetetus*.[2] It is to be noted that the Greek conception of the *bánausos* (the common working man), as might easily be shown from the above quotation from Plato, means not only an uneducated man, a man insensitive to poetry and art, and with no spiritual view of the world, but further-

62

more a man who lives by manual labour as distinguished from the man who owns sufficient property to dispose freely of his time. Here, once again, does it not appear as though our thesis implied a return to the Greek notion of the common working man and to the social and educational conceptions of the pre-Christian era? Certainly not! Yet is this not implicit in the refusal to accept the term 'work' (which, as has always been said, is supposed to be a term of praise) as applying to the *whole* sphere of man's intellectual and spiritual activity? On the contrary, in my opinion everything must be done, on the one hand to obliterate a contrast of this kind between the classes, but on the other hand it is quite wrong, and indeed foolish, to attempt to achieve that aim by looking for social unity in what is (for the moment!) the purely terminological reduction of the educated stratum to proletarian level, instead of the real abolition of the proletariat. What do we mean, fundamentally, by the words 'proletariat', and 'deproletarianization'?—It will be as well, in attempting to answer the question and to define the terms, to leave firmly aside all discussion of the practicability of 'deproletarianizing', in order to answer the question purely 'theoretically' and from the point of view of the principles involved.

In the first place, a proletarian and a poor man are not the same. A man may be poor without being a proletarian: a beggar in medieval society was certainly not a proletarian. Equally, a proletarian is not necessarily poor: a mechanic, a 'specialist' or a 'technician' in 'totalitarian work state' is certainly a proletarian. Secondly, this, though obvious, has to be said: the negative aspect of the notion 'proletariat', the thing to be got rid of, does not consist in the fact that it is a condition limited to a particular stratum of society; so that the negative aspect would disappear once *all* had become proletarians. 'Proletarianism' cannot obviously be overcome by making everyone proletarian.

What, then, is proletarianism? If the numerous sociological definitions and terms are reduced to a common denominator, the result might be expressed in the following terms: the proletarian is the man who is fettered to the process of work.

This still leaves the phrase 'process of work' vague and in need of clarification. It does not, of course, mean work in the ordinary sense: the never-ceasing activity of man. 'Process of work', here, means useful work in the sense already defined, of contributing to the general need, to the *bonum utile*. And so 'process of work' means the all-embracing process in which things are used for the sake of the public need. To be fettered to work means to be bound to this vast utilitarian process in which our needs are satisfied, and, what is more, tied to such an extent that the life of the working man is wholly consumed in it.

To be tied in this way may be the result of various causes. The cause may be lack of property: everyone who is a propertyless wage-earner is a proletarian, everyone 'who owns nothing but his power to work',[3] and who is consequently compelled to sell his capacity to work, is a proletarian. But to be tied to work may also be the consequence of a ukase in a totalitarian labour state: in this case everyone (whether he owns property or not) who is utterly subjected 'to the necessities of an absolute economic process of production,'[4] by outside forces, which means that he is entirely subject to economic forces, is a proletarian.

In the third place, to be tied to the process of work may be ultimately due to the inner impoverishment of the individual: in this context everyone whose life is completely filled by his work (in the special sense of the word work) is a proletarian because his life has shrunk inwardly, and contracted, with the result that he can no longer act significantly outside his work, and perhaps can no longer even conceive of such a thing.

Finally, all these different forms of proletarianism, particularly the last two, mutually attract one another and in so doing intensify each other. The 'total work' State needs the spiritually impoverished, one-track mind of the 'functionary'; and he, in his turn, is naturally inclined to find complete satisfaction in his 'service' and thereby achieves the illusion of a life fulfilled, which he acknowledges and willingly accepts.

This inner constraint, the inner chains which fetter us to 'work', prompts a further question: 'proletarianism' thus understood, is perhaps a symptomatic state of mind common to *all* levels of society and by no means confined to the 'proletariat', to the 'worker', a *general* symptom that is merely found isolated in unusually acute form in the proletariat; so that it might be asked whether we are not all of us proletarians and all of us, consequently, ripe and ready to fall into the hands of some collective labour State and be at its disposal as functionaries—even though explicitly of the contrary political opinion. In that case, spiritual immunization against the seductive appeal and the power of totalitarian forms must, surely, be sought and hoped for at a much deeper level of thought than on the level of purely political considerations?[5]

In this context the distinction between the liberal and the servile arts acquires a fresh significance. In antiquity and the Middle Ages, the essence of the *artes serviles* was held to consist in their being directed, as St. Thomas says, 'to the satisfaction of a need through activity'. 'Proletarianism' would then mean the limitation of existence and activity to the sphere of the *artes serviles*—whether this limitation were occasioned by lack of property, State compulsion, or spiritual impoverishment. By the same token, 'deproletarianizing' would mean: enlarging the scope of life beyond the confines of merely useful servile work, and widening the sphere of servile work to the advantage of the liberal arts; and this process, once again, can only be carried out by combining three things: by giving the wage-earner the opportunity to save and acquire property, by limiting the power of the state, and by overcoming the inner impoverishment of the individual.

If this process is to be successful—and 'deproletarianization' must not be confused with the struggle against poverty (so urgent that no word need be lost on that score)—then it must be assumed that the distinction between the *artes liberales* and the *artes serviles* is a real one, i.e. it must be recognized that there is a real distinction between useful activity on the one hand, the sense and purpose of which is not in itself, and on the other hand the liberal arts which cannot be put at the disposal of useful ends. And it is entirely consistent that those who stand for the 'proletarianizing' of everyone, should deny all meaning to the distinction and try to prove that it has no basis in reality.

To take an example: the distinction between the liberal arts and the servile arts runs parallel with the terms: honorarium and wage. Properly speaking, the liberal arts receive an honorarium, while servile work receives a wage. The existence of these words implies that in the first instance there exists some incommensurability between the performance and the reward and that the performance cannot, rightly speaking, be paid for. A 'wage', on the contrary (understood in contradistinction to honorarium), implies payment for good work, and that the performance can be valued in terms of money: work and wage are

67

not incommensurable. Furthermore honorarium means a contribution towards the cost of living, whereas a wage (in the above narrower sense) means payment for a particular piece of work, with no reference to the needs of the individual concerned. Now it is very significant that the extreme Marxist type of intelligence does not recognize the difference between honorarium and wage: all payment is in the form of a wage. In a sort of manifesto on the situation of the author in society today,[6] in which literature is proclaimed a 'social function', Jean-Paul Sartre announces that the writer, who has in the past so seldom 'established a relation between his work and its material recompense', must learn to regard himself as 'a worker who receives the reward of his effort'. There, the incommensurability between the achievement and the reward, as it is implied and expressed in an 'honorarium', is declared non-existent even in the field of philosophy and poetry which are, on the contrary, simply 'intellectual work'. By contrast a social doctrine steeped in the tradition of Christian Europe would not only hold firmly to the distinction between an honorarium and a wage, it would not only hesitate to regard every reward as a wage; it would go further and would even maintain that there is no such thing as a recompense for a thing done which did not retain in some degree the character (whether much or little) of an honorarium, for even 'servile' work cannot be entirely equated with the material recompense because it is a 'human' action, so that it always retains something incommensurable with the recompense—just like the liberal arts.

And so it comes about, paradoxical though it may seem, that the proletarian dictator Stalin should say: 'The worker must be paid according to the work done and not according to his needs,'[7] and that the Encyclical 'Quadragesimo anno' which has for one of its principal aims the 'deproletarianizing' of the masses, should assert that 'in the first place the worker has the right to a wage sufficient to support himself and his family.'[8] On the one hand, there is an attempt to restrict and even to extirpate the liberal arts: it is alleged that only useful, 'paying' work makes sense; on the other hand, there is an attempt to extend the character of 'liberal art' deep down into every human action, even the humblest servile work. The former aims at making all men into proletarians, the latter at 'deproletarianizing' the masses.

There is, however, a fact which from the vantage-point we have now reached must be strikingly clear and significant, and it is this: whereas the 'total work' State declares all un-useful work 'undesirable', and even expropriates free time in the service of work, there is one Institution in the world which forbids useful activity, and servile work, on particular days, and in this way prepares, as it were, a sphere for a non-proletarian existence.

Thus one of the first socialists, P. J. Proudhon (whom

Marx dismissed as a 'petit bourgeois')[9] was not so far wrong in beginning his work with a pamphlet on the celebration of Sunday, the social significance of which he expresses in the following words: 'On one day in the week servants regained the dignity of human beings, and stood again on a level with their masters.'[10] And in the introduction to his little book, Proudhon gets very near to the heart of the matter when he says, 'Discussion about work and wages, organization and industry, which is so rife at present ought, it seems to me, to start with the study of a law which would have as its basis a theory of rest.'[11] It is true that the full meaning of this 'theory of rest' is not open to one who, like Proudhon, examines it exclusively 'from the point of view of public health, morality, the family and social conditions.' And here is something to be examined more closely.

Let us begin by summing up what has already been said in this excursus: If the essence of 'proletarian' is the fact of being fettered to the process of work, then the central problem of liberating men from this condition lies in making a whole field of significant activity available and open to the working man—of activity which is *not* 'work'; in other words: in making the sphere of real leisure available to him.

This end cannot be attained by purely political measures and by widening and, in that sense, 'freeing' the life of the individual economically. Although this would entail much that is necessary, the essential

70

would still be wanting. The provision of an external opportunity for leisure is not enough; it can only be fruitful if the man himself is capable of leisure and can, as we say, 'occupy his leisure', or (as the Greeks still more clearly say) *skolen agein*, 'work his leisure' (this usage brings out very clearly the by no means 'leisurely' character of leisure).

'That is the principal point: with what kind of activity is man to occupy his leisure'[12]—who would suspect that that was a sentence taken from the *Politics* of Aristotle? What, then, ultimately makes leisure inwardly possible and, at the same time, what is its real justification?

*

It is time to return to the question: can the realm of leisure be saved and its foundations assured by an appeal to *humanism*? On closer inspection it will be seen that 'humanism', understood as a mere appeal to a *humanum*, does not serve.

The soul of leisure, it can be said, lies in 'celebration'. Celebration is the point at which the three elements of leisure emerge together: effortlessness, calm and relaxation, and its superiority to all and every function.

But if 'celebration' is the core of leisure, then leisure can only be made possible and indeed justifiable upon the same basis as the celebration of a feast: and that formation is *divine worship*.

There is no such thing as a feast 'without Gods'—

71

whether it be a carnival or a marriage. There is no such thing as a feast that does not ultimately derive its life from divine worship, and that does not draw its vitality as a feast from divine worship. That is not a demand or a requirement; it does not mean that that is how things *ought* to be. It claims to be a simple statement of fact: however dim the recollection of the association may have become in men's minds, a feast 'without Gods', and unrelated to worship, is quite simply unknown. It is true that ever since the French Revolution attempts have repeatedly been made to manufacture feast-days and holidays that have no connection with divine worship, or are some-times even opposed to it: 'Brutus days', or even that hybrid 'Labour Day'. In point of fact the stress and strain of giving them some kind of festal appearance is one of the very best proofs of the significance of divine worship for a feast; and nothing illustrates so clearly that festivity is only possible where divine worship is still a vital act—and nothing shows this so clearly as a comparison between a living and deeply traditional feast day, with its roots in divine worship, and one of those rootless celebrations, carefully and unspontaneously prepared beforehand, and as arti-ficial as a maypole.

All this is true too of leisure: its possibility, its ulti-mate justification derive from its roots in divine worship. That is not a conceptual abstraction, but the simple truth as may be seen from the history of religion.

What does a 'day of rest' mean in the Bible, and for that matter in Greece and Rome? To rest from work means that time is reserved for divine worship: certain days and times are set aside and transferred to 'the exclusive property of the Gods'.[13]

Divine worship means the same thing where time is concerned, as the temple where space is concerned. 'Temple' means (as may be seen from the original sense of the word): that a particular piece of ground is specially reserved, and marked off from the remainder of the land which is used either for agriculture or for habitation. And this plot of land is transferred to the estate of the Gods, it is neither lived on, nor cultivated. And similarly in divine worship a certain definite space of *time* is set aside from working hours and days, a limited time, specially marked off—and like the space allotted to the temple, is not *used*, is withdrawn from all merely utilitarian ends. Every seventh day is a period of time of that kind: that is what a feast is, and such is its only origin and justification.

There can be no such thing in the world of 'total labour' as space which is not used *on principle*; no such thing as a plot of ground, or a period of time withdrawn from use. There is in fact no *room* in the world of 'total labour' either for divine worship, or for a feast: because the 'worker's' world, the world of 'labour' rests solely upon the principle of rational utilization. A 'feast-day' in that world is either a pause in the midst of work (and for the sake of work, of course), or in the case of 'Labour Day', or whatever feast days of the world of 'work' may be called, it is the very principle of work that is being celebrated— once again, work stops for the sake of work, and the feast is subordinated to 'work'. There can of course be games, *circenses*, circuses—but who would think of describing that kind of mass entertainment as festal?

It simply cannot be otherwise: the world of 'work' and of the 'worker' is a poor, impoverished world, be it ever so rich in material goods; for on an exclusively utilitarian basis, on the basis, that is, of the world of 'work', genuine wealth, wealth which implies over-flowing into superfluities, into unnecessaries, is just not possible. Wherever the superfluous makes its appearance it is immediately subjected to the rationalist, utilitarian principle of the world of work. And, as the traditional Russian saying puts it: work does not make one rich, but round-shouldered.

On the other hand, divine worship, of its very nature, creates a sphere of real wealth and superfluity, even in the midst of the direst material want—because sacrifice is the living heart of worship. And what does sacrifice mean? It means a free offering freely given and *never* anything useful or utilitarian; in fact it means the very opposite of 'using' and 'useful'. And thus by means of active participation in the sacrifice of the *cultus* a capital wealth is created which the

74

world of work can never consume, a super-abundance
of wealth that cannot be calculated, and that the
fluctuations of the world of trade never can disturb—
a real wealth, overflowing and superfluous, neither
tied nor limited by end or aim: the holiday and feast.
That is the sphere (both spatial and temporal) in
which leisure unfolds itself and comes to fruition.

Separated from the sphere of divine worship, of the
cult of the divine, and from the power it radiates,
leisure is as impossible as the celebration of a feast.
Cut off from the worship of the divine, leisure becomes
laziness and work inhuman.

That is the origin or source of all sham forms of
leisure with their strong family resemblance to want
of leisure and to sloth (in its old metaphysical and
theological sense). The opportunity is given for the
mere killing of time, and for boredom with its marked
similarity to the inability to enjoy leisure; for one can
only be bored if the spiritual power to enjoy leisure,
or if you prefer, to be leisurely, has died away. There
is an entry in Baudelaire's *Journal Intime* that is
fearful in the precision of its cynicism: 'One must
work, if not from taste then at least from despair. For,
to reduce everything to a single truth: work is less
boring than pleasure.'

And the counterpart to that is the fact that if
real leisure is deprived of the support of genuine feast-
days and holy-days, work itself becomes inhuman:
whether endured brutishly or 'heroically' work is

naked toil and effort without hope—it can only be compared to the labours of Sisyphus, that mythical symbol of the 'worker' chained to his function, never pausing in his work, and never gathering any fruit from his labours.

In its extreme form the passion for work, naturally blind to every form of divine worship and often inimical to it, turns abruptly into its contrary, and work becomes a cult, becomes a religion. To work means to pray, Carlyle wrote, and he went on to say that fundamentally all genuine work is religion, and any religion that is not work ought to be left to Brahmins and dancing dervishes. Could anyone really pretend that that exotic 19th-century opinion was merely *bizarre* and not much more nearly a charter for the world of 'total work'—that is on the way to becoming our world?

The celebration of divine worship, then, is the deepest of the springs by which leisure is fed and continues to be vital—though it must be remembered that leisure embraces everything which, without being *merely* useful, is an essential part of a full human existence.

In a period when divine worship is deeply felt and unites the whole social body and is, moreover, acknowledged as valid by all or nearly all, it might (perhaps) not be quite so necessary to discuss the ingredients of leisure explicitly; and in so far as it was necessary to justify leisure in such periods it might (perhaps) be enough to dwell upon the purely humanistic arguments. But at a time when the nature of culture is no longer even understood, at a time when 'the world of work' claims to include the whole field of human existence, and to be co-terminous with it, it is necessary to go back to fundamentals in order to rediscover the ultimate justification of leisure.

An appeal to antiquity in the name of learning merely is virtually meaningless in times such as these; it is powerless against the enormous *pressure*, internal as well as external, of 'the world of work'. An appeal to Plato is no longer any good—unless one goes to the very roots of Plato (for we are concerned with roots, not with precedents, 'influences'). Nor is it any use emphasizing that the traditions of philosophy go back to Plato's Academy, unless at the same time one accepts the religious character of the original 'academy'; for Plato's academy was a religious association with its own divine worship, in which the *cultus* was of such importance that we find it explicitly laid down that one of its members should be appointed to prepare the sacrifice. Perhaps the reason why 'purely academic' has sunk to mean something sterile, pointless and unreal is *because* the *schola* has lost its roots in religion and in divine worship. And so, instead of reality we get a world of make-believe, of intellectual *trompe l'œil*, and cultural tricks and traps and jokes, with here and there a 'temple of the Muses' and a 'holy of holies'. Goethe certainly seems to have thought as much when he referred to the classicism of his day, in an astonishing phrase, declaring all the '*inventa* of antiquity' to be 'matters *of faith*' which are now 'fantastically copied out of pure fantasy'.[14]

To repeat: today it is quite futile to defend the sphere of leisure in the last ditch but one. The sphere of leisure, it has already been said, is no less than the sphere of culture in so far as that word means everything that lies beyond the utilitarian world. Culture lives on religion through divine worship. And when culture itself is endangered, and leisure is called in question, there is only one thing to be done: to go back to the first and original source.

Such is, moreover, the meaning of the marvellous quotation from Plato placed at the beginning of this essay. The origin of the arts in worship, and of leisure derived from its celebration, is given in the form of a magnificent mythical image: man attains his true form and his upright attitude 'in festive companionship with the Gods'.

But what—someone may well ask—are we *to do* about it?

Well, the considerations put forward in this essay were not designed to give advice and draw up a line of action; they were meant to make men think. Their aim has been to throw a little light on a problem which seems to me very important and very urgent, and is all too easily lost to sight among the immediate tasks in hand.

The object of this essay, then, is not to provide an immediate, practical guide to action. Nevertheless, there is one hope which ought, in conclusion, to be set down clearly—the fact is that in this sphere the decisive result is not to be achieved through action but can only be hoped for.

Our hope is, in the first place, that the many signs *intra et extra muros* of a re-awakening of the feeling for worship and its significance should not prove deceptive and misleading. For, to recapitulate: no one need expect a genuine religious worship, a *cultus*, to arise on purely human foundations, on foundations made by man; it is of the very nature of religious worship that its origin lies in a divine ordinance, a fact which is moreover implied in the quotation from Plato already referred to. No doubt the feeling for what has been ordained and laid down may increase, or it may lose its vitality. And that is the point towards which our hopes are directed—and not, of course, to the revival of some antiquated cult; and still less towards the foundation of a new religion! From those who see no hope along these lines (and hopelessness along these lines, it must be conceded, could produce not a few grounds in its defence)—from those who see nothing worth hoping for here—we should certainly not expect to find confidence in the future. This is a matter about which it seems to me of the utmost importance to leave no doubt in their minds.

Worship is either something 'given', divine worship

is fore-ordained—or it does not exist at all. There can be no question of founding a religion or instituting a religious *cultus*. And for the Christian there is, of course, no doubt in the matter: *post Christum* there is only *one*, true and final form of celebrating divine worship, the sacramental sacrifice of the Christian Church. And moreover I think that anyone enquiring into the facts of the case from an historical point of view (whether he is a Christian or not) would be unable to find any other worship whatsoever in the Europeanized world.

The Christian *cultus*, unlike any other, is at once a sacrifice and a sacrament.[15] In so far as the Christian *cultus* is a *sacrifice* held in the midst of the creation which is affirmed by this sacrifice of the God-man —every day is a feast-day; and in fact the liturgy knows only feast-days, even working days being *feria*. In so far as the *cultus* is a *sacrament* it is celebrated in visible signs. And the full power of worship will only be felt if its sacramental character is realized in undiminished form, i.e. if the sign is fully visible. In leisure, as was said, man oversteps the frontiers of the everyday workaday world, not in external effort and strain, but as though lifted above it in ecstasy. That is the sense of the visibility of the sacrament: that it should be the means of lifting man out of himself, so that he is rapt to the heavens. Let no one imagine for a moment that that is a private and romantic interpretation. The Church has pointed to the meaning of the incarnation of the Logos in the self-same words: *ut dum visibiliter Deum cognoscimus, per hunc in invisibilium amorem rapiamur*, that we may be rapt into love of the invisible reality through the visibility of that first and ultimate sacrament: the Incarnation.

Now, our hope is that the true sense of sacramental visibility in the celebration of the Christian *cultus* should become manifest to the extent needed for drawing the man in us, who is 'born to work', out of himself, and should draw him out of the toil and moil of every day into the sphere of unending holiday, and should draw him out of the narrow and confined sphere of work and labour into the heart and centre of creation.

NOTES

The quotation preceding the essay is from the *Laws* (653 C-d). The psalm is translated from the Septuagint; it begins with the word σχολάσατε. It has been said by Joseph Bernhardt that this verse 'became an axiom of mystical epistemology'.

I

1. In his well-known study on Capitalism and Protestant ethics, p. 171 (1934).
2. *Nicomachean Ethics*.
3. *Politics*, 8, 3 (1337 b).
4. Ernst Niekisch, *Die dritte imperiale Figur* (1935).
5. Ernst Jünger, *Der Arbeiter. Herschaft und Gestalt* (1932).

II

1. *Blätter und Steine*, p. 202 (1934).
2. Bernhard Jansen, *Die Geschichte der Erkenntnislehre in der neueren Philosophie*, p. 235 (1940).
3. "Von einem neuerdings erhobenen vornehmen Ton in der Philosophie." *Akademie-Ausgabe*, VIII, pp. 387–406.
4. Fragment 112 (Diels).
5. *Quaest. disp. de veritate*, 15, 1.
6. *Quaest. disp. de virtutibus cardinalibus*, 1.

7. Kant, *loc. cit.*

8. *Maximen und Reflexionen*, No. 1415 (edition Günther Müller, 1943).

9. Hermann Rauschning, *Gespräche mit Hitler* (Zürich, 1940).

10. Loc. cit., p. 390.

11. Schiller, *Die Philosophen.*

12. Found in Diogenes Laertius, *The Lives and Opinions of Renowned Philosophers*, VI, Book I, Cap. 2.

13. Ibid. One of Antisthenes's works bears the title *The Greater Hercules, or Of Power.*

14. Anton Gail has drawn my attention to the fact that in a portrait of Erasmus by Holbein (at Longford Castle) Erasmus's hands are resting on a book in which are to be read the words: 'Herakleou ponoi—Erasmi Roterodami'.

15. Carlyle, quoted by Robert Langewiesche.

16. Cf. Wiehelm Nestle: *Griechische Geistesgeschichte von Homer bis Lukian*, 1944, pp. 313 ff.

17. Ibid., p. 314.

18. Quoted by Clement of Alexandria.

19. Cf. Diogenes Laertius, VI, 1.5.

20. *Summa Theologica*, II, ii, 123, 12 ad 2.

21. Ibid., II, ii, 27, 8 ad 2.

22. Ibid., II, ii, 108, 2

23. *Quaest. disp. de caritate*, 8 ad 17.

24. Commentary on Proverbs, 1, d. 2 (expositio tertus).

25. Ernst Jünger, *Blätter und Steine*, p. 179.

26. *Summa Theologica*, II, ii, 141, 5 ad 1.

27. *Summa Contra Gentes*, 4, 23; cf. also *Summa Theologica*, 1, 38, 2 ad 1.

28. *Summa Theologica*, I, 21, 14.

29. Commentary on the *Metaphysics*, I, 3.

30. Newman: *Idea of a University*, V, 6.

31. Ibid.

32. *Blätter und Steine*, p. 176.

33. Quoted in Eckermann's *Conversations*.

34. Commentary on Proverbs.

III

1. See Joseph Pieper, *Über die Hoffnung*, p. 55.

2. *Sickness unto Death*, pp. 74 ff.

3. *Quaest. disp. de malo*, 11, 3.

4. W. Sombart, *Der Bourgeois*, pp. 322, 313, 321 (1913).

5. Max Scheler, *Vom Umsturz der Werte*, Vol. II, p. 293 (1919).

6. Johannes Haessle, *Das Arbeitsethos der Kirche nach Thomas von Aquin und Leo XIII*, p. 31 (1923).

7. *De unitate intellectus*.

8. Johannes Haessle, loc. cit.

9. *Summa Theologica*, II, ii, 35, 3 ad 1; *Quaest. disp. de malo*, 11, 3 ad 2.

10. In the entry dated 12 Sept. 1939.

11. Fragment 75 (Diels).

12. Karl Kerényi, *Die antike Religion*, p. 66 (1940).

13. *Summa contra Gentes*, II, 96.
14. Richard Wright in *Die Umschau*, Vol. I, Heft 2, pp. 214–16.
15. Nicomachean Ethics, 10, 7 (1177b).

IV

1. Trübner's *Deutsches Wörterbuch* (Berlin, 1939).
2. *Theaetetus*, 175 f.
3. Pius XI, The Encyclical 'Quadragesimo anno'.
4. Ibid.
5. Although in writing *Thesen zur sozialen Politik* (first published in 1933). I *expressly* limited myself to the consideration of political questions, and was therefore aware of the limitations of a purely political view, I now regard the essay as requiring completion at many points. It is surely characteristic of the generation formed between the wars that they expected in general too much from unadulterated politics.
6. Published in the first number of *Les Temps Modernes*.
7. Stalin in a public statement made in 1933.
8. 'Quadragesimo anno', pp. 55 ff.
9. P. T. Proudhon, *Die Sonntagsfeier, aus dem Gesichtspunkt des öffentlichen Gesundheitswesens, der Moral, der Familien- und bürgerlichen Ver hältnisse betrachtet* (Kassel, 1850).
10. Ibid., p. 18.

11. Ibid., p. vi.
12. Aristotle, *Politics*, 8, 3 (1337 b).
13. *Reallexikon für Antike und Christentum*, 1942
    Article "Arbeitsruhe".
14. Goethe to Riemer, 26 March 1814.
15. *Summa Theologica*, III, 79, 5.

THE
PHILOSOPHICAL ACT

The reason, however, why the philosopher may be likened to the poet is this: both are concerned with the marvellous.

THOMAS AQUINAS

I

When a physicist sets out to define his science and asks what physics is, he is posing a preliminary question; in asking it he is plainly not at the experimental stage—not yet, or perhaps, no longer. But for anyone to ask, What does philosophizing mean? is quite certainly philosophy. The question is neither a preliminary one, nor is it just a postscript, one to be raised after the task has been accomplished—in some such form as: 'What have we been doing?' The question occurs in the very midst of the undertaking. More precisely, I can say nothing whatsoever about philosophy without simultaneously saying something about man and his nature—and that, after all, is one of the central matters of philosophy. The opening question, What does philosophizing mean? is certainly philosophical.

But like all philosophical questions, it cannot be answered with complete finality. The answers to philosophical questions cannot, of their nature, be what Parmenides called 'neatly rounded truths' and they cannot be picked and held in the hand like apples. The whole structure of philosophy and of philosophizing is different: it is a structure conditioned by hope; on which point there will be something to say later.

As a preliminary approach, however, it may be said that to philosophize is to act in such a way that one steps out of the world of work in which man earns bread by the sweat of his brow. The next thing to do is to define what is meant by the workaday world, and then what is meant by going beyond that sphere.

The workaday world is the world of work, the utilitarian world, the world of the useful, subject to ends, open to achievement and sub-divided according to functions; it is the world of supply and demand, of our needs and their satisfaction. It is dominated by a single end: the satisfaction of the 'common need'; it is the world of work in so far as work is synonymous with useful activity (which in addition is characterized by being toil). Work is the process of satisfying the 'common need'—an expression that is by no means synonymous with the notion of 'common good'. The 'common need' is an essential part of the 'common good'; but the notion of 'common good' is far more comprehensive. For example, the 'common good' requires (as Aquinas says[1]) that there should be men who devote themselves to the 'useless' life of contemplation, and, equally, that some men should philosophize—whereas it could not be said that contemplation or philosophy helps to satisfy the 'common need'.

More and more, at the present time, 'common good' and 'common need' are identified; and (what comes

90

to the same thing) the world of work is becoming our entire world; it threatens to engulf us completely, and the demands of the world of work become greater and greater, till at last they make a 'total' claim upon the whole of human nature.

If, then, it is true to say that in the act of philosophizing we transcend the world of work and are carried beyond the world of work, it becomes plain that the question 'What does philosophizing mean?', which sounds so innocent at first, so 'theoretical', so abstract, is a very pressing and 'actual' question at the present time. There is only one step in thought (and geographically too) to finding ourselves in a world where work, labour, the process of satisfying the 'common need', give their impress to the whole of human existence; inwardly as well as outwardly, the frontier between us and the world of 'total work' is pressing in upon us—a world in which there is no room for philosophy or philosophizing in any true sense of the word: always assuming, of course, that to philosophize means to transcend the workaday world and that the philosophical act is incommensurable with the world of supply and demand, and the world of the 'common need', and belongs elsewhere. And in fact, the more 'total' the demands of the world of work, the more sharply and clearly do we see that philosophy is incommensurable with it. It may even be said that philosophy is conditioned at the present time by this situation and by the threat of the world of 'total work', even more decisively than by its own proper problems. Philosophy—inevitably—becomes more and more distant, strange and remote; it even assumes the appearance of an intellectual luxury, and is felt to be a load on the social conscience, as the workaday world extends its claims and its sway over man.

The incommensurability of the philosophical act and the sphere of the workaday world needs, however, to be seen in its concrete aspects. It does not require any great effort of imagination to bring vividly to mind the things that dominate everyday life: we are plunged drastically in their midst. For so many people there is the daily struggle for a bare physical existence, for food, warmth, clothing and a roof over their head. In addition to our private worries and anxieties, and naturally influencing them, there is the need for reconstruction in Europe especially and more particularly in Germany—and the call for the organization of a new world. And alongside all this there is the struggle of nations for the goods of the earth. Everywhere there is a feeling of strain, of being overwrought and over-done—and this fatigue is only relieved in appearance by the breathless amusements or the brief pauses that punctuate its course: newspapers, a cinema, a cigarette. I do not have to detail what everyone knows. But there is no need either to concentrate on the present-day crisis and on the exaggerations which that involves. I mean quite simply the ordinary everyday world in which we live and play our part, with its very concrete ends to be achieved and realized, and which have to be squarely faced. Nothing, in fact, is further from my intention than in any way whatsoever to denigrate this world as though from some supposedly superior 'philosophical' standpoint. Not a word need be wasted on that subject; that world is of course essentially part of man's world, being the very ground of his physical existence—without which, obviously, no one could philosophize!

But all the same, just try to imagine that all of a sudden, among the myriad voices in the factories and on the market square (Where can we get this, that or the other?)—that all of a sudden among those familiar voices and questions another voice were to be raised, asking: 'Why, after all, should there be such a thing as being? Why not just nothing?'—the age-old, philosophical cry of wonder that Heidegger[2] calls the basic metaphysical question! Is it really necessary to emphasize how incommensurable philosophical enquiry and the world of work are? Anyone who asked that question without warning in the company of people whose minds hinge on necessities and material success would most likely be regarded as crazy. It is, however, in extreme cases such as this that the whole extent of the contrast comes to light: and then it is clear that the question transcends the workaday world and leads beyond it.

A properly philosophical question always pierces the dome that encloses the bourgeois workaday world, though it is not the only way of taking a step beyond that world. Poetry no less than philosophy is incommensurable with it.

> *How sweet I roam'd from field to field*
> *And tasted all the summer's pride,*
> *Till I the Prince of love beheld*
> *Who in the sunny beams did glide!* [3]

Surely the sudden effect of poetry in the realm of means and ends comes as strange and remote as a philosophical question. Nor is it otherwise with prayer. Perhaps it is still understandable that men should say: 'Give us this day our daily bread', but what of the words of the *Gloria*: *Gratias agimus tibi propter magnam gloriam tuam?*—can words such as these be understood in the context of the 'rational-useful' and of a utilitarian organization? Man also steps beyond the chain of ends and means, that binds the world of work, in love, or when he takes a step towards the frontier of existence, deeply moved by some existential experience, for this, too, sends a tremor through the world of relationships, whatever the occasion may be— perhaps the close proximity of death.

Indeed, not only the act of philosophizing, but every genuine experience (and like the act of philosophizing, poetry and the aesthetic experience, as well as prayer spring from some 'disturbance') is an experience of the non-finality of this worried, troubled world: then man transcends that world or takes a step beyond it.

The philosophical act, the religious act, the aesthetic act, and, of course, the effect of love and death, or some other way in which man's relation to the world is convulsed and shaken—all these fundamental ways of acting belong naturally together, by reason of the power which they have in common of enabling a man to break through and transcend the workaday world.

Plato, as everyone knows, virtually identified philosophy and Eros. And in regard to the similarity of philosophy and poetry, there is the little-known and curious saying of Aquinas which occurs in his commentary on the *Metaphysics* of Aristotle: The philosopher, he there says, is related to the poet in that both are concerned with *mirandum*, with wonder, with marvelling and with that which makes us marvel.[4] That saying is not altogether easily plumbed, and it acquires added significance because, as thinkers, Aristotle and Aquinas are both cool-headed, sensible men, altogether averse from any kind of romantic blurring of the orders. Thus poetry and philosophy are more closely related to one another than any of the sciences to philosophy; both, equally, are aimed, as one might say, at wonder (and wonder does not occur in the workaday world)—and this by virtue of the power of transcending the everyday world, a power common to poetry and philosophy. But to that we shall return again.

The family resemblance between all these acts is so significant and of such importance that whenever *one* member is denied in principle, the remainder cannot live—and in a totalitarian world of work every form and manner of transcendence is bound to wither (would perish, indeed, if human nature could be destroyed or altered entirely): for where the religious spirit is not tolerated, where there is no room for poetry and art, where love and death are robbed of all significant effect and reduced to the level of a banality, philosophy will never prosper.

But worse, even, than the silencing or simple extinction of these experiences of transcendence is their transformation, their degradation, into sham and spurious forms; and pseudo-realizations of these fundamental acts most certainly exist, giving the appearance of piercing the dome of everyday life. It is possible to pray in such a way that one does not transcend the world, in such a way that the divine is degraded to a functional part of the workaday world. Religion can be debased into magic. Then it is no longer devotion to the divine, but an attempt to master it. Prayer can be perverted in this way, into a sort of technique whereby life under the dome is feasible. Moreover, there is, too, a perversion of Eros in which all the powers of devotion are bent to serve a narrow and confined ego, a perversion that results from anxiously preserving oneself from being moved by the world into which love alone can lead us. Then again, there is a pseudo-art and a spurious poetry which, instead of bursting through the dome, merely paints and decorates its inner surface, as it were, either in a private or in a political capacity. These shams produce a poetry and an art that are 'useful' to the workaday world: the sort of poetry that never pierces the dome— and, of course, genuine philosophy has far more in common with the exact sciences than with any pseudo-poetry. And finally, there is even a pseudo-philosophy, and its mark is the same: it does not transcend the workaday world. At one point, it will be remembered, Socrates asks Protagoras the Sophist[5], 'What do you really teach the young who crowd to your lectures?', and Protagoras replies: 'To be well informed—both in their own affairs, namely how best to manage one's house and run one's estate, and in matters concerning the State; how best to be effective in speaking and in acting.' That is the classical programme of philosophy considered as a profession, as training: a pseudo-philosophy that will never pierce the dome.

And the worst of it all is, that these spurious forms combine—not indeed to go beyond the workaday world, but on the contrary—to screw down the dome more firmly than ever, to close every window—and then man really is imprisoned in the world of work. These deceptive forms, and of them all a spurious philosophy is the worst, are much more harmful, much more hopeless than the naïve self-sufficiency of the man who excludes the very possibility of anything not fitting perfectly into the everyday, workaday world. Nevertheless a man who is thus caught up and entwined in the strands of everyday life may still be shaken, one day, by some profound emotion, whether it comes to him in the form of a philosophical question, or a poem, or a face; but a pseudo-philosopher, a sophist, never!

Turning again to the question we began with, if we enquire into the real nature of philosophy, we are asking a question which goes beyond the workaday world and even makes it questionable. It is very evident that the present time adds point to the question, to the doubt if you like; for when, in the whole course of European history, has the world of work made so totalitarian a claim as it makes today? Nevertheless, this is not intended as a critique of the present age; the problem is a fundamental one and it is our business to clarify, not a new but an ever present confusion of thought.

When the Thracian Maid saw Thales of Miletus, the star-gazer, fall into the cistern she laughed; and Plato accepted her laughter as the answer of hard-headed common sense to philosophy. The history of European philosophy might be said to begin with that legend. Ever and again, so we are told in the *Theae-tetus*, 'ever and again' the philosopher is the occasion of laughter: 'not only the Maids of Thrace, but the many laugh at him because, a stranger to the world, he falls into a cistern as, indeed, into embarrassment.'[6]

Now in order to convey his inmost thoughts Plato does not express himself only, or even mainly, in explicit words or in formal theses; he tends to use the characters of the dialogues almost dramatically. There is, for instance, Apollodorus, a subsidiary character in the *Phaidon* and the *Symposium*, as one might easily be led to suppose. Apollodorus is one of those uncritical, enthusiastic youngsters who follow in the wake of Socrates and who are, perhaps, intended to suggest Plato himself as a young man. We are told in the *Phaidon* that when Socrates drank the hemlock, Apollodorus was the only one present to burst into tears: 'of course you know him and his way of carrying on.'[7] In the *Symposium*,[8] Apollodorus himself recounts how, for years, he had been eager to know what Socrates had said and done each day; 'formerly I went about, driven along by events, and thought I was being very busy, while all the time I was more wretched than anyone'. Then he met Socrates, and devoted himself whole-heartedly to him and to philosophy. The whole town began to talk of him as 'crazed'; he got furious with everyone, and even with himself, with the exception always of Socrates. He went about everywhere, naïvely announcing that he was 'happy beyond all measure' as long as he could talk about philosophy or hear others talk about it; and then grew miserable at failing to achieve his ambition and be like Socrates.

Then, one day, Apollodorus meets some old friends, the very ones in fact, who call him mad. And, as Plato is careful to note, they are business men, only interested in money, who know how to make and produce things, and who are convinced that they are 'getting things done'. These friends of his, nevertheless, ask Apollodorus to tell them something about the banquet that was held in the poet Agathon's house, and the speeches on love that followed. It is clear enough that these business men, with their belief in success, felt not the least need to be instructed in the meaning of the world and existence—least of all by Apollodorus. All they cared about, probably, was the wit and elegance of the speeches, a well-turned phrase or a delicate innuendo. Nor, for the matter of that, has Apollodorus any illusion about their 'philosophical leanings'. Quite the reverse. He says straight out that he is sorry for them—'because you think you are doing something when you are really doing nothing. Now, you may, perhaps, think that I am badly off, and I dare say you are right on that score; but I not only believe you are badly off: I know it for certain.' But all the same, he is not afraid of telling them what was said: he simply cannot keep quiet: 'if you really want to know, then I must tell you'—even though it confirms them in thinking him crazy. And then Apollodorus tells them—the *Symposium*! The *Symposium* is a story told by Apollodorus in indirect speech. I cannot help feeling that too little attention is paid to the fact that Plato puts his profoundest thoughts into the mouth of an enthusiast, an over-zealous, uncritical, somewhat fantastic youngster, hardly more than an undergraduate—and what is more before an audience of hardheaded business men who were neither capable nor, indeed, desirous, of taking what was said seriously. There is an element of hopelessness, of despair almost, about the situation—and Plato's meaning seems to be that, faced with that situation, only the unflinching eagerness of youth in its search for wisdom could hope to prevail: a situation in which only a genuine *philosophia* could survive. But however that may be, Plato could not have emphasized the incommensurability of philosophizing and the self-sufficient world of work more plainly.

But that is only the negative aspect of the incommensurability in question; the other aspect is: freedom. Philosophy is 'useless' and unusable in matters of everyday life where things are to be turned to account and results achieved: that is one point. It is quite another thing, however, to say that it serves no purpose whatsoever beyond itself and its own end or that it can never be used apart from its own end. Philosophy is not functional knowledge but, as Newman said, 'the knowledge of a gentleman';[9] not a useful knowledge, but a 'free' knowledge. Freedom, here, means that philosophical knowledge is not legitimized by its usefulness or usableness, or by virtue of its social function, or with reference to the 'common need'. This is the self-same sense in which 'freedom' was used in the phrase 'artes liberales', the liberal arts—in contradistinction to the 'artes serviles', the servile arts which, as Aquinas says, are 'ordered to the satisfaction of a need through activity'.[10] Philosophy has always been regarded as the freest of all the liberal arts (and in the Middle Ages the philosophical faculty was even named after the artes liberales: ordo artistarum, the faculty of liberal arts).

And so it comes to the same thing if I say that the act of philosophizing transcends the world of work, or or if I say that philosophical knowledge is unusable, or if I call philosophy a 'liberal art'.

The special sciences, it should be noted, are only free in this sense in so far as they are pursued philosophically. That is actually, as well as historically, the meaning of academic freedom (for academic, in this case, means philosophical or it means nothing); and any claim to academic freedom, in the strict sense of the word, can only arise in so far as 'academic' fulfils its philosophical character. And actually, as well as historically, academic freedom goes by the board in exactly the same degree in which the philosophical character of academic studies is lost; in other words, to the extent to which the total claim of the world of work invades the academic sphere. That is the metaphysical root of the matter; and the so-called 'political' invasion is only a consequence and a symptom.

It should, however, most certainly be added that this failure is the direct fruit of philosophy itself, of modern philosophy. And with one more word on that subject, we will conclude this chapter.

But first, one word on the freedom of philosophy,

as distinguished from the sciences: 'freedom' being understood to mean 'not being at the disposal of external aims and ends'. The different branches of science are 'free' in this sense, provided only that they are pursued philosophically and in so far as they share the freedom of philosophy. 'Knowledge is free,' writes Newman, 'in the truest sense, as soon as and in so far as it is philosophical.'[11] In themselves, however, the various branches of science may perfectly well be placed 'at the disposal of external aims and ends', and they can always be 'applied' in order to satisfy a need (which is Aquinas's definition of a servile art).

To take a concrete example. The government of a country may quite well say: 'In order to carry out our five-year plan, we need physicists trained in these particular branches of their science, men who will help to put us ahead of other countries'; or: 'We need medical research students to discover a more efficient cure for the 'flu.' Something of this kind may happen, and still it could not be said that there was any essential interference with the science in question. But: 'At the moment we need philosophers to . . .'— well, what? There is of course only one conclusion—'to elaborate, defend and demonstrate the following ideology'—it is only possible to talk or write in such terms if philosophy is being strangled to death at the very same moment. Exactly the same thing would be true if someone in authority were to say: 'At the moment, we need some poets to . . .'—well, and 'to what?' And again, there is only one possible answer: to prove (as the saying goes) the pen mightier than the sword in the service of some idea dictated by the state. And that, obviously, is the death of poetry. The moment such a thing happened, poetry would cease to be poetry, and philosophy would cease to be philosophy.

But this is not to say that there is no sort of connection between the fulfilment of the 'common good' and the philosophy taught in a country! Only the relationship can never be established or regulated from the point of view of the general good: when a thing contains its own end, or is an end in itself, it can never be made to serve as a means to any other end—just as no one can love someone 'in order that'.

The fact that philosophy cannot be put at the disposal of some end other than its own is intimately connected with its theoretical character and is, indeed, identical with it—and that is a point which is of the greatest importance, which ought to be stressed. To philosophize is the purest form of *speculari*, of *theorein*, it means to look at reality purely receptively—in such a way that things are the measure and the soul is exclusively receptive. Whenever we look at being philosophically, we discourse purely 'theoretically' about it, in a manner, that is to say, untouched in any way whatsoever by practical considerations, by the desire to change it; and it is in this sense that philosophy is said to be above any and every 'purpose'.

The realization of 'theorizing', in this sense, is however, closely connected with a prior attitude of mind. It assumes the prior existence of a certain relation to the world, a relation prior to any conscious construction and foundation. We can only be theoretical in the full sense of the word (where it means a receptive vision untouched by the smallest intention to alter things, and even a complete readiness to make the will's consent or dissent dependent upon the reality we perceive through the recognition of which we give our yea or our nay)—we can only be 'theoretical' in this undiluted sense, so long as the world is something other (and something more) than a field for human activity, its material, or even its raw material. We can only be 'theoretical' in the full sense of the word if we are able to look upon the world as the creation of an absolute spirit.

There is, then, a quite definite relationship to the world that is the only soil in which 'pure theory' can live. The freedom to philosophize and of philosophy itself, are both bound to that assumption, to that relationship, as by the firmest of ties. Nor is it to be wondered that the collapse of that relation to reality and the weakening of that tie (by virtue of which the world is viewed as a Creation and not as material for man to act upon) should keep pace with the collapse of the theoretical character of philosophy, with the loss of its superiority to a mere function, and with the decay of philosophy itself. There is a direct link

105

between 'Knowledge is power', or Bacon's other statement, that the purpose of knowledge is to furnish man with new inventions and gadgets[12]—and Descartes's blunt statement of his aim in the *Discourse*, of replacing theoretical philosophy, in order to become the 'masters and owners of nature'[13]—and on to Marx's well-known formula: up to the present philosophy has been concerned with interpreting the world, whereas it ought to be busy altering it.

Historically speaking, the path which leads down to the suicide of philosophy is this—once the world begins to be looked upon merely as the raw material of human activity, it is only a step to the abolition of the theoretical character of philosophy. Once the world ceases to be looked upon as created, theory in the full sense of the word becomes impossible. The loss of 'theoria' means *eo ipso* the loss of the freedom of philosophy: philosophy then becomes a function within society, solely practical, and it must of course justify its existence and role among the functions of society; and finally, in spite of its name, it appears as a form of work or even of 'labour'. Whereas my thesis (which should by now be emerging plainly with its contours well defined), is that the essence of 'philosophizing' is that it transcends the world of work. It is a thesis which comprehends the assertion of the theoretical character of philosophy and its freedom; it does not, of course, in any way deny or ignore the world of work (indeed it assumes its prior and necessary existence), but it does affirm that a real philosophy is grounded in belief, that man's real wealth consists, not in satisfying his needs, not in becoming 'the master and owner of nature', but in seeing what is and the whole of what is, in seeing things not as useful or useless, serviceable or not, but simply as being. The basis of this conception of philosophy is the conviction that the greatness of man consists in his being *capax universi*.[14]

The ultimate perfection attainable to us, in the minds of the philosophers of Greece, was this: that the order of the whole of existing things should be inscribed in our souls. And this conception was afterwards absorbed into the Christian tradition in the conception of the beatific vision: 'What do they not see, who see Him who sees all things?'[15]

II

To philosophize, then, is to take a step beyond the everyday world of work.

Now the meaning of a step is best defined in relation to its goal, to the 'whither' rather than to the 'whence'. Where does philosophizing carry us? Obviously, in going beyond the world of work, it crosses a frontier: what sort of a world lies beyond? And how are the two worlds related, the world into which the act of philosophizing carries us, and the world which this same act transcends? Could it be said that the former is the 'essential' world, and the world of work the inessential; is it the 'whole' as opposed to the part; or is it reality as contrasted with appearance?

However these questions may be answered in detail, one thing is clear: both worlds, the world of work and the realm into which the act of philosophizing carries us—*both* belong to the world of man which is clearly, therefore, a many-storied structure.

Our next question, then, is: What kind of a world is man's world?—a question which patently cannot be answered without reference to the nature of man. And in order to achieve some degree of clarity, we must begin from the beginning and start from the bottom.

Every living thing lives in a world, in 'its' world, and 'has' a world in which it lives. To live means to be 'in' the world. Though a stone, you may say, is surely 'in' the world? Everything there 'is', is 'in' the world, surely? But let us stick to the stone, for the moment, lifeless, lying about with other things, next to other things and surely 'in' the world. 'In', 'next to', 'with', all prepositions, words indicating a relation: though the stone is not really related to the world 'in' which it is, nor to the things 'next to' which it lies, nor to those 'with' which it is in the world. A relationship in the proper sense of the word, is a link established from inside to something external; relations can only exist where there is an 'inside', where there is a dynamic centre from which all activity proceeds and to which everything in the nature of experience (which by contrast is passive) is referred. In this qualitative sense (one cannot, of course, speak of the 'inside' of a stone—one can only speak of the 'inside' of a stone with reference to the disposal of its parts), the 'inside' is the power by virtue of which a relation to something external is possible; inwardness is the capacity to establish relations and to communicate. And what of 'world'? Well, world means the same thing as a range of relations. Only a being capable of having relations, only a being of whom 'inner' as well as 'outer' may be predicated—and this in its turn means a living being—has a world. Only a living being exists within a range of relationships.

109

contra Whitehead.
Aquinas has natural
appetite,

There is a fundamental difference between relations thus conceived and the relation which results from the proximity of stones in a heap by the roadside, though technically one can, of course, speak of stones neighbouring one upon the other. That form of relation is, again, different from the relation between a plant and the nutriment it draws through its roots out of the ground, for then the relation is not solely spatial, an objective fact and nothing more, it is a real relation in the primary sense of the word, in the active reflexive sense of 'relating itself': the nourishment in the ground and in the air is absorbed and assimilated into the sphere of the plant's life by the dynamic centre of the plant, and its power of establishing relations. All that constitutes the plant's range of relations makes its world. A plant, in fact, has a world, and a stone has not.

That, then, is the first point: the world is a field of relations. To have a world is to be the centre, the co-ordinator, of a field of relations. The second point is: the higher the *order* of a being, the more embracing and wider its power of establishing relations—the greater the field of relations within its power. This may also be expressed by saying that the higher a being stands in the order of reality, in the hierarchic order of being, the wider and deeper its world.

The lowest world, the first step in the hierarchy, is that of the plant which does not extend its spatial world beyond the sphere of touch. The animal's world is higher than this and corresponds to the animal's greater power of establishing relations. The animal's capacity to establish relations is greater in so far as it is capable of being sensibly and sensually aware; 'to be aware' of a thing is an entirely new mode of relating itself to a thing, unknown in the plant world, a new manner of relating itself to the 'outside'.

It is by no means true, however, that everything an animal is able, abstractly speaking, to see or to hear, belongs to its 'world'; animals possessed of eyes do not actually see, nor could they see, everything that is visible in their 'surroundings'. And 'surroundings', even 'surroundings' which could 'in themselves' be apprehended, do not constitute a 'world'. Though this view was far from generally held until Jacob von Uexküll, the biologist, published his findings. Up to that time, as Uexküll himself puts it,[1] 'it was generally assumed that all animals with eyes saw the same objects'. But Uexküll found that this was far from being the case. 'The animal's "environment" is something altogether different from the natural scene; it more nearly resembles a small, poorly furnished room.'[2] And he gives the following example: one might have supposed that a jackdaw, 'with eyes in its head', could see a grasshopper (after all, a very desirable object to a jackdaw) at least when there was one before its eyes. But not at all! And here I will quote Uexküll:

'A jackdaw is utterly unable to see a grasshopper

that is not moving . . . We are perhaps inclined to suppose that although the shape of a grasshopper is familiar to the jackdaw, it is unable to recognize a grasshopper if a blade of grass cuts across it, it cannot recognize it as the 'unity' grasshopper—just as we find it quite difficult to recognize a familiar object in a picture-puzzle. On this assumption it is only when the grasshopper jumps that its shape becomes recognizable and dissociates itself from the surrounding images. But further experiments lead one to suppose that a jackdaw simply does not know the shape of a motionless grasshopper and is so constituted that it can only apprehend the moving form. That would explain why so many insects feign death. If their motionless form simply does not exist in the field of vision of their enemies, then by shamming death they drop out of that world with absolute certainty and cannot be found even though searched for.'[3]

Animals are perfectly adapted to their sharply defined and delimited environment—perfectly adapted to it, but equally, imprisoned within it, so that they cannot overstep the frontier in any way whatsoever: they cannot even find an object though armed with senses that are apparently well adapted to the purpose, unless, that is, the object fits completely into their selected, partial world. This selected reality, selected by the biological necessities either of the individual or the genus or species, so limited and sharply defined, is what Uexküll calls *Umwelt*: 'environment' in con-

trast to 'surroundings' and in contrast to 'world',
as appeared from the subsequent discussion of the
question. An animal's field of relationships is not its
'surroundings' and certainly not 'the world'. Its field
of relationships is a very clearly delimited 'environment': a world from which something has been
omitted, in which its inmate is enclosed and to which
it is, at the same time, perfectly adapted.

All this may seem, at first sight, somewhat distant
from the theme with which we began: 'What do we
mean by philosophizing?' But it is not simply a di-
gression. We had reached the point of asking about
man's world, and that is where Uexküll's conception
of 'environment' is relevant—for (according to Uexküll) our human world 'cannot claim to be any more
real than the animal's world'[4]; man, then, is limited by
his environment in exactly the same way as an animal,
that is to say, he is limited to a selected environment
assembled, as it were, by natural selection and biological necessity; he is incapable of apprehending anything and, even though searching for it, of finding
anything outside his environment—like the jackdaw
that cannot find a motionless grass-hopper. (The
question does arise, however, as to how a creature
limited to its own environment and imprisoned so
effectively within it could study the theory of environment. But that is a question which need not be pursued: it is better left on one side for the time being.)

The immediate problem dictated by the course of

this enquiry is man and his world: what sort of a capacity for relations does man possess, and what are his powers? It has already been said that, by comparison with plants, an animal's power of apprehension is radically new because it is wider and embraces far more. Now, man's characteristic form of apprehension is 'knowledge'—from time immemorial called 'spiritual knowledge'—and perhaps it is a further capacity for relations, more embracing than that of plant and animal life. To this essentially new capacity for relations there must, surely, correspond a field or world, of other dimensions no doubt, answering to that capacity. The answer to this question is that in the tradition of Western philosophy, the capacity for spiritual knowledge has always been understood to mean the power of establishing relations with the whole of reality, with all things existing; that is how it has been defined, and it is conceived as a definition more than as a description. *Spirit*, it might be said, is not only defined as incorporeal, but as the power and capacity to relate itself to the totality of being. *Spirit*, in fact, is a capacity for relations of such all-embracing power that its field of relations transcends the frontiers of all and any 'environment'. To talk of 'environment' where spirit is concerned, is a misunderstanding, for its field of relations is 'the world', and by its very nature it breaks the bounds of any 'environment', and this in both senses, as regards adaption and as regards imprisonment: and that is why spirit

114

makes man free, and why it requires him to 'venture'
and perhaps to venture all.

In summing up what he has said about the soul in
the *De anima*, Aristotle says:[5] 'The soul is, fundamentally, everything that is'—words which were to
become a favourite tag in the Middle Ages: *anima est
quodammodo omnia*, the soul is in a certain sense all
things, the all. 'In a certain sense' means to say in so
far as it knowingly places itself in relation to the whole
of being (and to know something means to become
identical with the known reality, though this is not
the place to say more on that score). The spiritual soul,
Aquinas says, in his considerations on truth, is meant
to fit in with all being, *convenire cum omni ente*.[6]
'Every other being takes only a limited part in being',
whereas the spiritual being is 'capable of grasping the
whole of being'.[7] And 'because there is spirit, it is
possible for the perfection of the whole of being to
exist in one being'.[8]

That is the tradition of Western philosophy: to
have spirit, or to be spirit, means to exist in the midst
of the whole of reality and before the whole of being,
the whole of being, *vis-à-vis de l'univers*. Spirit does
not exist in 'a' world, nor in 'its' world, but in 'the'
world, 'the' world in the sense of *visibilia omnia et
invisibilia*.

'The whole of reality' and 'spirit' are corresponding conceptions. One cannot have the one without the
other. The power or capacity to relate oneself to 'the'

115

world *is* spirit! And essentially speaking, spirit is the power to relate oneself to 'the' world.

In Plato, Aristotle, Augustine and Aquinas, in the philosophy of antiquity and of the Middle Ages, the concepts 'spirit' and 'world' (in the sense of the whole of reality) are not only interrelated, their correspondence is complete. Not only was spirit held to be 'a relation with all that exists', the reverse proposition was equally held to be true, and held to be true, what is more, in a quite literal sense which we find difficult to imagine: all things are essentially related to spirit. So that not only is the totality of things the field of relations of spirit—things of their very nature exist in the field of spiritual relations. Furthermore, in the philosophical tradition of which I am speaking, it comes to the same whether I say 'things have being' or whether I say 'things exist in the field of relationship of spirit'—this does not of course refer to some vague, abstract 'spirituality', but to a personal spirit and its capacity to establish relationships—and not to God only, but equally to the created human spirit.

That is what is meant by the proposition *omne ens est verum* (everything that is, is true)—though we have almost ceased to understand it—and by the complementary proposition that being and truth are interchangeable concepts. (What does truth mean, where things are concerned, the truth of things? 'A thing is true' means: it is known and knowable, known to the absolute spirit, knowable to the spirit that is not

116

absolute. Unfortunately I can only ask you to accept
that statement as it stands; this is not the place to
embark on its interpretation.[9] For our present purpose the important thing about the concept 'the
truth of things' is that it means that the essence of
things is to be related to spirit.)

To sum up: the world of a spiritual being is the
totality of existing things; and their correspondence
is so complete that it is both essential to spirit
(spirit is the power of embracing the totality of being)
and equally it is essential to things themselves ('to
be' means 'to be in relation to spirit').

We found, in the course of our considerations, a
hierarchic ladder of 'worlds' of which the world of
plants was the lowest, limited to the spatial, to the
things it touched; next comes the environment of
animals; and finally the world corresponding or co-
ordinated to spirit, that includes and transcends all
these other partial, limited worlds: *the* world as the
totality of being. And this hierarchy of worlds, of
fields of relations, corresponds, as we saw, to the hierarchy of the graduated powers and capacities to establish relations; so that the greater the capacity for
relations the greater the dimensions of the co-ordinated
field, until that field becomes (for spirit) 'the'
world.

To this double chain of steps or grades we must
now add a third, structural, element: the greater the

power of establishing relations the greater the degree of inwardness; the lowest degree of relations corresponds not only to the most limited world but also to the most restricted form of inwardness—while spirit, which corresponds to the totality of being, is also the highest form of inwardness, what Goethe called '*wohnen in sich selbst*'—dwelling in oneself. The more embracing the power with which to relate oneself to objective being, the more deeply that power needs to be anchored in the inner self of the subject so as to counterbalance the step it takes outside. And where this step attains a world that is in principle complete (with totality as its aim) the reflective self, characteristic of spirit, is also reached. The two together constitute spirit: not only the capacity to relate oneself to the whole of reality, to the whole world, but an unlimited capacity of living in oneself, the gift of self-reliance and independence that has always been regarded as the decisive element in personality in the philosophical tradition of Europe. To have a world, to be related to the whole of reality, is only possible to a self, to a person, to a 'who' and not to a 'what'.

It is now time we looked back again at the two questions we began with. There were two questions, an immediate and a wider: the immediate question concerned the nature of man's world and the wider question was 'what do we mean by philosophizing?'

Before taking them up again formally, there is just one more observation to be made on the structure of

the world in the context of 'spirit': it is not, of course,
merely in the matter of quantitative size that the
world in this context is differentiated from the 'environment' of plants and animals—a fact which so many
discussions about world and environment so often
overlook. The world co-ordinated to spirit is not
merely the world of all things but at the same time of
the essence of things. And that is why an animal's
environment is limited: because the essence of things
is concealed from it. And, contrariwise, it is only because man, being a spirit, is capable of attaining the
essence of things, that he can embrace the totality of
things—this interrelationship was traditionally expressed in the following terms: both the essence of
things and the universe is 'universal'; and in the
words of Aquinas, 'the spiritual soul is capable of the
infinite because it can grasp the universal'.[10] To know
the universal essence of things is to reach a point of
view from which the whole of being and all existing
things become visible; at the same time the spiritual
outpost thus reached by knowing the essence of things
enables man to look upon the landscape of the whole
universe.

But to return to the question, first of all the preliminary question about man's world. Is the world thus
co-ordinated to spirit, man's world? The answer to
this is that man's world is the whole of reality; man
lives in and is confronted by the whole of reality,
vis-à-vis de l'univers—in so far as he is spirit. But

119

not only is he not pure spirit, he is finite spirit; and consequently the essence of things and their totality is not given to him fully and completely in the purity of the concept: but 'in hope', and on that point I shall have something to add in the next chapter.

In the meanwhile let us consider the implications of saying that man is not pure spirit. It is a statement that can be made in different keys, with many variations of tone, so that the emphasis falls at a different point and strikes from a different angle—a note of regret, for instance, is by no manner of speaking unusual, and indeed Christians as well as non-Christians consider it 'quite specially Christian'. It can also be expressed so as to imply that while man is not pure spirit, the 'real man' is, 'of course', the spiritual soul. Neither tendency, however, has any ground in the Western tradition of Christendom. There is a passage in St. Thomas that points the argument with all desirable clarity. He puts to himself the following objection: The end of man is, surely, perfect similarity with God, and the soul separated from the body will be more like God than the soul joined to the body, since God is incorporeal. The soul in its final state of happiness, therefore, will be separated from the body. That is the objection Aquinas uses in order to introduce the thesis 'the real man is the spiritual soul', attired, as it were, in all the finery of a theological argument. To that objection he replies as follows: 'The soul united to the body is more like God than the soul separated from the body because it possesses its own nature more perfectly'[11]—an answer that is by no means easily digested, for it implies not only that man is corporeal, but that in a certain sense, even the soul is corporeal.

But if that be so, if man is *essentially* not pure spirit, not spirit only, and if man is a being in whom plant, animal and spiritual life are fused together and thus fused not merely as the consequence of some failure on his part to attain his end, of some lagging behind his destiny—if that be so, then he cannot be expected to live exclusively or essentially face to face with the whole world of reality; on the contrary, he must live in a field of relationships where world and environment are necessarily incorporated, one within the other, and corresponding to the complex nature of man (as opposed to the simple nature of animal or pure spirit).

That is why man cannot live permanently 'beneath the stars', *vis-à-vis de l'univers*; he needs the roof of the familiar over his head, the surroundings of everyday life, the sensual proximity of the concrete, the regularity of habit and custom. In a word: a full human life calls for environment, too, in the differentiated sense we have given it, in which environment is not 'the world'.

At the same time it is one of the characteristics of man, a corporeal and spiritual being, that it should be his spiritual soul which informs the physical and sensitive realms—to such a degree that taking food in man and animal are two utterly different things (quite apart from the fact that in the human sphere a 'meal' may have a spiritual or even a religious character). It is so true that the spiritual soul informs the whole of man's nature that even when a man 'vegetates' it is ultimately only possible because he is spiritual—a cabbage can't vegetate. Equally, when man shuts himself up in his environment, in the sphere defined and limited by his immediate needs, the degeneration that follows is only possible because spiritual degeneration is possible. The really human thing is to see the stars above the roof, to preserve our apprehension of the universality of things in the midst of the habits of daily life, and to see 'the world' above and beyond our immediate environment.

And with that we are back unawares at our first question: 'What do we mean by philosophizing?' It means to experience the fact that our immediate surroundings, prescribed as they are by the aims and needs of life, not only can be, but must be broken in upon (not only once but ever and again), by the disturbing call of 'the world', of the whole world and the everlasting and essential images of things mirrored by reality. To philosophize—and what we asked was whither the philosophical act carries us when it transcends the workaday world—to philosophize means to step beyond the sectional, partial environment of the workaday world into a position *vis-à-vis de l'uni-*

vers: a step that takes one into the open, for the
heavens are not a roof over a man's head—though
one ought always to leave the door open behind one,
for a man cannot live like that continuously. Who, in
fact, would want to emigrate for good and all out of
the Thracian maid's world or think it possible to do so:
for it would mean leaving the human world altogether.
And in fact one could apply to philosophizing the
words that Aquinas used of contemplation when he
spoke of it as something really superhuman: *non
proprie humana, sed superhumana.*[12] To be sure, man
himself, is in a measure superhuman and is, as Pascal
says, infinitely above man (every attempt to provide a
smooth definition of man is bound to fail).

But this is not the place to pursue a thought that
threatens to topple us over into enthusiasm. Our
question is 'what do we mean by philosophizing',
and it is that question we want to answer, quite
concretely and simply, and helped thereto by all that
we have already said. What distinguishes a philosophical question from one which is not philosophical?
To philosophize, we said, meant fixing our mind's eye
on the totality of being, 'the world'. Now, is *the*
philosophical question (and it alone) the question
which explicitly and formally concerns the totality of
being and of things? Of course not. But it is certainly
true that the distinctive mark of a philosophical
question is that it cannot be put, or weighed, or
answered (in so far as an answer is possible at all)

without bringing into play 'God and the world', without implied reference to all that is.

Let us take a concrete example. The question 'what are we doing, here and now?' can obviously be taken in a number of different ways; it *can* be given a philosophical meaning. It can have a purely superficial relevancy, concerned solely with a technical answer that deals with organization.'What is taking place here?'—'A philosophical lecture in the Summer School held at Bonn.' That is a clear statement in a perfectly clear, limited and fully illuminated framework. It is an answer given with an eye on our immediate surroundings. But the question can also be meant differently and the questioner might not be satisfied with the answer given. 'What is taking place here?'—One person is speaking, others are listening to the spoken word, and the hearers 'understand' what is said; and among the hearers roughly the same thing happens; what is said is apprehended, weighed, considered, accepted or rejected, introduced into each individual's mind and way of thought. This question may aim at a scientific answer, it may be given such a meaning that physiology and psychology (awareness, understanding, learning, memorizing, forgetting, etc.) are called upon to answer and are sufficient for the task. And that answer would certainly be given in a world of wider and deeper dimensions than the former answer, that was purely technical. But the various scientific answers are not given with reference to the whole of reality; they could be given without bringing in 'God and the world'. Yet, if the question 'what are we doing here and now?' is intended philosophically, to avoid that question would be impossible; if that is how the question is meant, then the question raises at the same time the meaning of knowledge, of truth or perhaps only of teaching. What in fact do we really mean by teaching? One man will maintain that no one can really teach, just as in the case of good health it is not the doctor who performs the cure, but nature whose healing powers the doctor has simply liberated (perhaps). Another man will maintain that it is God and God only who teaches one inwardly—using the occasion of human teaching. And along comes Socrates and says that the teacher only induces the learner to remember 'and to win knowledge from out of himself'; 'there is no such thing as learning, one only remembers once again'.[13] Yet another man comes along maintaining that we are all faced by or face the same reality: the teacher only points it out, the learner, the hearer, then sees it for himself.

'What are we doing here?' Something that takes place within the framework of a series of lectures, something organized; something moreover that can be grasped physiologically and psychologically and studied; something, too, between God and the world.

The distinctive mark of a philosophical question is,

then, that it brings out what constitutes the essence of spirit: *convenire cum omni ente*, in harmony with everything that is. One cannot ask a philosophical question or think philosophically without bringing the whole of being into play, the totality of existing things, 'God and the world'.

III

It is appropriate to the human situation, as we have
seen, not only for man to adapt himself to his environment, he must also address himself to the task of
seeing the world as a whole. And the act of philosophizing means that he transcends his environment and
steps forth into 'the world'.

That must not, of course, be understood to mean
that there are, as it were, two distinct, separate
spheres, and as though man could take leave of one
and enter the other. Nor is it true that there are things
which could be defined as belonging in his environment and others that do not occur in his environment,
but occur in the other sphere, 'the world'. Obviously,
our environment and the world (in the sense we have
given these terms) are not distinct and separate
spheres of reality—as though by asking a philosophical
question one moved from the first to the second. A
man philosophizing does not look away from his
environment in the process of transcending it; he
does not turn away from the ordinary things of the
workaday world, from the concrete, useful handy
things of everyday life; he does not have to look in
the opposite direction to perceive the universal world

of essences. On the contrary, it is the same tangible, visible world that lies before him upon which a genuine philosophical reflection is trained. But this world of things in their interrelationships has to be questioned in a specific manner: things are questioned regarding their ultimate nature and their universal essence, and as a result the horizon of the question becomes the horizon of reality as a whole. A philosophical question is always about some quite definite thing, straight in front of us; it is not concerned with something beyond the world or beyond our experience of everyday life. Yet, it asks what 'this' really *is*, ultimately. The philosopher, Plato says,[1] does not want to know whether I have been unjust to you in this particular matter, or you to me, but what justice really is, and injustice; not whether a king who owns great wealth is happy or not, but what authority is, and happiness and misery—in themselves and ultimately.

Philosophical questions, then, are certainly concerned with the everyday things that are before our very eyes. But to anyone raising such a question the things 'before his eyes' become, all at once, transparent, they lose their density and solidity and their apparent finality—they can no longer be taken for granted. Things then assume a strange, new, and deeper aspect. Socrates, who questioned men in this way, so as to strip things of their everyday character, compared himself for that reason to an electric fish that gives a paralysing shock to anyone who touches it. All day and every day we speak of 'my' friend, of 'my' wife, of 'my' house taking for granted that we 'have' or 'own' such things; then all of a sudden we are brought to a halt: do we really 'have' or 'own' all these things? Can anyone have such things? And anyway, what do we mean here by 'having' and 'owning' something?

To philosophize means to withdraw—not from the things of everyday life—but from the currently accepted meaning attached to them, or to question the value placed upon them. This does not, of course, take place by virtue of some decision to differentiate our attitude from that of others and to see things 'differently', but because, quite suddenly, things themselves assume a different aspect. Really the situation is this: the deeper aspects of reality are apprehended in the ordinary things of everyday life and not in a sphere cut off and segregated from it, the sphere of the 'essential' or whatever it may be called; it is in the things we come across in the experience of everyday life that the unusual emerges, and we no longer take them for granted—and that situation corresponds with the inner experience which has always been regarded as the beginning of philosophy: the act of 'marvelling'.

'By all the Gods, Socrates, I really cannot stop marvelling at the significance of these things, and at moments I grow positively giddy when I look at them', as the young mathematician *Theaetetus* impulsively declares, after Socrates has brought him to the point of admitting his ignorance, with his shrewd and kindly, but staggering and astonishing questions—questions that stagger and astonish one with wonder. And then follows Socrates's ironical answer: 'Yes, that is the very frame of mind that constitutes the philosopher, that and nothing else is the beginning of philosophy'.[2] There, for the first time, in the *Theaetetus*, without solemnity or ceremony, almost 'by the way', though fresh as dawn, appears the thought that has become a commonplace in the history of philosophy: the beginning of philosophy is wonder.

It is at this point that the thoroughly 'unbourgeois' character of philosophy emerges—if I may for a moment, and without an altogether good conscience, make use of a terminology that has become all too common. Yet wonder really is unbourgeois. For what do we mean by saying, in a spiritual sense, that something is bourgeois? Above all, in the first place, that a man accepts his environment defined as it is by the immediate needs of life, so completely and finally, that things happening cannot any longer become transparent; the great, wide, not to say deep, world which is at first sight invisible, the world of essences and universals, is not even suspected; nothing wonderful ever happens in this world, and wonder itself is unknown or lost. The narrow insensitive mind, that has become narrow through being insensitive, takes everything for granted. And what, in truth, is to be taken for granted? Are we to take our very existence for granted? Is the existence of 'sight' or 'perception' to be taken for granted? No one imprisoned in every-day life *can* ask such questions because, in the first place, he is unable to forget his immediate needs (not at any rate while in full possession of his senses, at very most in some half-stupefied state); whereas that is precisely what characterizes the man capable of won-der. Those who are struck by the deeper aspect of things find the immediate aims of life vanishing before them—even though only for so long as their vision of the face of the world moves them to wonder.

The unique and original relation to being that Plato calls 'theoria' can only be realized in its pure state through the sense of wonder, in that purely receptive attitude to reality, undisturbed and un-sullied by the interjection of the will. 'Theoria' is only possible in so far as man is not blind to the wonderful fact that things are. For our sense of won-der, in the philosophical meaning of the word, is not aroused by enormous, sensational things—though that is what a dulled sensibility requires to provoke it to a sort of *ersatz* experience of wonder. A man who needs the unusual to make him 'wonder' shows that he has lost the capacity to find the true answer to the wonder of being. The itch for sensation, even though disguised in the mask of *Bohème*, is a sure indi-cation of a bourgeois mind and a deadened sense of wonder.

To perceive all that is unusual and exceptional, all that is wonderful, in the midst of the ordinary things of everyday life, is the beginning of philosophy. And that, as both Aristotle and Aquinas, observe, is how philosophy and poetry are related. And Goethe, in his seventieth year, ended one of his short poems, *Parabase*, with the words: *Zum Erstaunen bin ich da*, which might be rendered by saying 'marvel is my *raison d'être*'. Ten years later Eckermann[3] records him saying that 'the very summit of man's attainment is the capacity to marvel'.

The philosopher and the poet are 'unbourgeois' in so far as they preserve a deep and strong sense of wonder, and this fact naturally exposes them to the danger of losing their foot-hold in the everyday world. Indeed it might almost be said that 'to be a stranger in the world' is their occupational disease (though of course there could no more be a professional philosopher than there could be a professional poet—for as we said, man *cannot* live permanently at such heights). Wonder, however, does not make a man 'able'—it means, after all, to be profoundly moved and 'shaken'. And those who undertake to live under the sign and constellation 'wonder' (why *is* there such a thing as being?) must certainly be prepared to find themselves lost, at times, in the ordinary workaday world. The man to whom everything is an occasion of wonder will sometimes simply forget to use these things in a workaday way.

But however that may be, it remains true that the capacity to wonder is among man's greatest gifts. To Aquinas it even appeared to offer proof that man could only find peace and rest in the contemplation of God; and conversely, because man's mind is ordained to knowledge of the first cause of the world, he is capable of wonder. Furthermore, Aquinas held that man's first experience of wonder sets his feet on the ladder that leads up to the beatific vision. And the truth that human nature is intended for no less an end is revealed in the fact that we are capable of experiencing the wonder of the creation, or quite simply that we are capable of wonder.

Wonder acts upon a man like a shock, he is 'moved' and 'shaken', and in the dislocation that succeeds all that he had taken for granted as being natural or self-evident loses its compact solidity and obviousness; he is literally dislocated and no longer knows where he is. If this were only to involve the man of action in all of us, so that a man only lost his sense of the certainty of everyday life, it would be relatively harmless; but the ground quakes beneath his feet in a far more dangerous sense, and it is his whole spiritual nature, his capacity to know, that is threatened.

It is an extremely curious fact that this is the only aspect of wonder, or almost the only aspect, that comes to evidence in modern philosophy, and the old view that wonder was the beginning of philosophy takes on a new meaning: doubt is the beginning of philosophy.

In one of Hegel's lectures on the history of philosophy[4] he speaks of Socrates's method and of how, in the dialogues, he excites his opponent to wonder *vis-à-vis* all that he had hitherto taken for granted, But, says Hegel, the confusion Socrates introduces into his opponent's mind is the principal thing: 'that purely negative thing is the main point', and further, 'confusion is what philosophy must begin with, and it produces that by itself; one must doubt everything, give up all one's assumptions, in order to receive it all (one's previous knowledge, etc.) back again by means of the concept.' And the line of descent from this position to Windelband's famous *Introduction to Philosophy* is unbroken. There, Windelband translates '$\theta\alpha\nu\mu\acute{\alpha}\zeta\epsilon\iota\nu$' boldly as 'Irrewerden des Denkens an sich selbst',[5] 'Thought becoming confused at itself.' Chesterton, be it said by the way, made a very pertinent comment on all such attempts to do without assumptions, when he said that there was a particular form of madness which consisted in losing everything but one's reason.

But does the true sense of wonder really lie in uprooting the mind and plunging it in doubt? Doesn't it really lie in making it possible and indeed necessary to strike yet deeper roots? The sense of wonder certainly deprives the mind of those penultimate certainties that we had up till then taken for granted—and to that extent wonder is a form of disillusionment, though even that has its positive aspect, since it means being freed from an illusion; and it becomes clear that what we had taken for granted was not ultimately self-evident. But further than that, wonder signifies that the world is profounder, more all-embracing and mysterious than the logic of everyday reason had taught us to believe. The innermost meaning of wonder is fulfilled in a deepened sense of mystery. It does not end in doubt, but is the awakening of the knowledge that being, *qua* being, is mysterious and inconceivable, and that it is a mystery in the full sense of the word: neither a dead end, nor a contradiction, nor even something impenetrable and dark; mystery really means that a reality, the singular existing thing, is inconceivable *because* it is an inexhaustible source of light, and for ever unfathomable. And that is the fact which is experienced in wonder.

It will now be seen that wonder and philosophy are related in a far more essential way than might, at first sight, be supposed from the saying that 'wonder is the beginning of philosophy'. Wonder is not just the starting point of philosophy in the sense of *initium*, of a prelude or preface. Wonder is the *principium*, the lasting source, the *fons et origo*, the immanent origin of philosophy. The philosopher does not cease 'wondering' at a certain point in his philosophizing—he does not cease to wonder unless, of course he ceases to philosophize in the true sense of the word.

The inner form of philosophizing is virtually identical with the inner form of wonder. And since we have asked 'what we mean by philosophizing' we must now enquire more closely into the nature of wonder.

There is something about wonder which is both positive and negative. The negative aspect is this: to wonder is not to know fully, not to conceive absolutely; it means not to know what is behind it all; it means, as Aquinas says, 'that the cause of our wonder is hidden from us'.[6] And so, to wonder is not to know, not to know fully, not to be able to conceive. To conceive a thing, to possess comprehensive and exhaustive knowledge of a thing, is to cease to wonder. It cannot therefore be said that God 'wonders'—because the knowledge of God is perfect. But, furthermore, to wonder is not merely not to know; it means to be inwardly aware and sure that one does not know, and that one understands oneself in not knowing. And yet it is not the ignorance of resignation. On the contrary to wonder is to be on the way, *in via*; it certainly means to be struck dumb, momentarily, but equally it means that one is searching for the truth. In the *Summa Theologica*[7] wonder is defined as the *desiderium sciendi*, the longing for knowledge, an active desire for knowledge. Although to wonder means, as we have said, not to know, it does not mean that we are, in a kind of despair, resigned to ignorance. Out of wonder, says, Aristotle,[8] comes joy. In this he was followed by the Middle Ages: *omnia admirabilia sunt delectabilia*,[9] so that joy and wonder are produced by the same things. Perhaps one might risk the following proposition:

Wherever there is spiritual joy, wonder will also be found; and wherever the capacity for joy exists the capacity for wonder will be found. The joy that accompanies wonder is the joy of the beginner, of the mind and spirit that is always open to what is fresh, new, and as yet unknown.

In its fusion of positive and negative, of ignorance on the way to further knowledge, wonder reveals itself as having the same structure as hope, the same architecture as hope—the structure that characterizes philosophy and, indeed, human existence itself. We are essentially *viatores*, on the way, beings who are 'not yet'. Who could claim to possess the being intended for him? 'We are not,' says Pascal, 'we hope to be.' And it is because the structure of wonder is that of hope that it is so essentially human and so essential to a human existence.

The philosophy of antiquity looked upon wonder as decisively and exclusively human. The absolute spirit does not wonder because untouched by the negative, for there is no ignorance in God. Only a being who does not know fully can wonder. But equally animals can have no sense of wonder because, as Aquinas says, 'the sensual soul is not drawn to undertake the search for causes',[10] because the positive element in 'the structure of wonder' (corresponding to hope) is absent: the desire for knowledge. It is only someone who *does not yet* know fully who 'wonders'. Wonder, in fact, was accepted so instinctively as

137

essential to a human life that in the quarrels and discussions that centred on Christological doctrine there
was an argument in favour of the full humanity of
Christ which might be called 'an argument from
wonder'. Arius had denied the divinity of Christ;
whereas Apollinaris put forward the thesis that the
eternal Logos had taken the place of the spiritual soul
in Christ and had immediately assumed a human body.
We are not concerned here with the theological side,
though it is in this kind of theological connection that
one finds the traditional doctrine of being expressing
itself 'under oath', as it were. In his argument against
the teaching of Apollinaris that Christ did not possess
the full humanity of body and soul (but of body only)
Thomas Aquinas argues, among other things, from
wonder: we are told in Holy Scripture, in the story of
the centurion (Luke vii, 9), that 'Christ wondered':
'Lord I am not worthy, say but the word . . .', upon
which, the Gospel tells us, ' Jesus heard and marvelled '
—$\epsilon\theta\alpha\acute{\upsilon}\mu\alpha\sigma\epsilon\nu$. But if Jesus could 'marvel', Aquinas
says,[11] we must suppose the presence of that which is
capable of marvel, of the *mens humana*, the human
mind, of the spiritual soul in addition to the presence
of the Divine Word and the sensual soul (both of
which are, as we have seen, not capable of 'wonder').
Only a spiritual capacity for knowledge that does
not know everything it knows at once and perfectly
is capable of becoming gradually aware of the
deeper and more essential world behind the sensual,

physical world—only the human spirit is capable of wonder.

It is this distinctively human gift which is the mark of philosophy. The Gods, we are told by Diotima in the *Symposium*,[12] do not philosophize; neither Gods nor fools, for 'the really damaging thing about stupidity is its self-satisfaction'. 'Who then, Diotima, I [Socrates] asked, who then philosophizes, if neither the wise nor the foolish philosophize? And to that she answered: It must surely be clear, even to a child, that it is those who are between the two, in the middle'. The 'middle' is the truly human sphere. The truly human thing is neither to conceive or comprehend (like God), nor to harden and dry up; neither to shut oneself up in the supposedly clear and enlightened everyday world, nor to resign oneself to remaining ignorant; not to lose the childlike suppleness of hope, the freedom of movement that belongs to those who hope.

And so the man who philosophizes and 'wonders' is ultimately superior to the man who is dulled by despair and narrowed by dullness—by virtue of his hope. And it is because he is far from finally possessing full and complete knowledge that he must continue to hope, to wonder and to philosophize.

It is, among other things, because it has the same structure as hope, that philosophy is radically different from the sciences. In philosophy and in science, the object is regarded in a radically different manner.

The questions which science asks can all of them, in principle, be fully answered, or at any rate they are not unanswerable in principle. The cause of a specific infection will, or could, one day be given. In principle it will one day be possible to say: it has now been definitely, scientifically established that this and nothing else is the case. A philosophical question, on the other hand, can never be finally answered and disposed of—for instance 'what *is* this, ultimately?' or 'what is illness?' or 'what is knowledge?' or 'what is man?' 'No philosopher', we find Aquinas saying,[13] 'has ever been able to grasp the being of a single fly', though, to be sure, it is counterbalanced by the other statement that in knowledge, the mind drives forward to the essence of things.[14] The object of philosophy is given to the philosopher 'in hope'. And here Dilthey's words might be recalled: The demands made upon anyone philosophizing, he wrote, are quite unrealizable. A physicist is a delightful reality, useful to himself and to others; the philosopher, like the saint, exists only in the ideal.[15]

The sciences, it could be said, cease of their nature to wonder—to the extent to which they attain results. To philosophize simply means to go on 'wondering'.

This gives us a clear picture of the greatness and the frontiers of science, and simultaneously the rank and questionableness of philosophy. True enough, in itself it is nobler to live under the open sky. But no man can stand it uninterruptedly. True enough, too,

140

a question aimed at the universe as a whole and at the ultimate essence of things, is higher in rank than any scientific question. Only . . . the answer is quite simply not within our reach in the same way that the answers to a scientific question are.

Since the very beginning philosophy has always been characterized by hope. Philosophy never claimed to be a superior form of knowledge but, on the contrary, a form of humility, and restrained, and conscious of this restraint and humility in relation to knowledge. The words philosopher and philosophy were coined, according to legend—and the legend is of great antiquity—by Pythagoras in explicit contrast to the words *sophia* and *sophos*: no man is wise, and no man 'knows'; God alone is wise and all-knowing. At the very most a man might call himself a lover of wisdom and a seeker after knowledge—a philosopher. Plato speaks in the same tone in the *Phaedrus*[16] where he asks what we ought to call Solon and Homer; and Socrates there decides that 'to call him wise seems to me, O Phaedrus, altogether too much, for it is only applicable to a God; but a philosopher, one who loves and seeks wisdom, or something of the kind, seems to me suitable.'

These stories are, of course, well known. But we are prone to regard them as mere anecdotes, as no more than rather special forms of expression, interesting to the student of language. Yet it seems to me that there is ample ground for attending very carefully to the implications which the study of words reveals.

But what, exactly, is the import of these anecdotes? There are two things to note. The first point is that we do not possess knowledge or wisdom which is the end and aim of philosophical enquiry; and moreover, that not only do we not possess it at the moment, or by chance, but on the contrary, that we *cannot* in fact have it, and that we are dealing with a perpetual 'not yet'.

To enquire about the essence of a thing implies a claim to be able to comprehend it. Now, to comprehend a thing means, according to Aquinas, to know it as fully and as completely as it can be known; it means to transform all that can be known into knowledge, to know something through and through, to the utmost limits of its knowability.[17] But there is absolutely nothing that man can know in this way, in the strict sense of the word 'comprehend'. No question concerning the essence of things, and that means no philosophical question, can, therefore, be answered in the exact sense in which they are asked. Philosophy, in fact, aims at a type of wisdom which is unattainable, though not, of course, in such a way that it has no relation whatsoever to its aim. It is simply that wisdom is the object of philosophy, but as lovingly sought, and never fully possessed.

That is the first thing expressed by the word philosophy as it was used by Pythagoras, Socrates and Plato. This meaning was adopted by Aristotle and developed further in his *Metaphysics*. It subsequently passed from Aristotle, though with some variation, to the great medieval thinkers. Aquinas's commentary on the *Metaphysics* of Aristotle, for instance, contains some very surprising and penetrating remarks on this theme. Among other things, he says that because wisdom is sought for its own sake, it cannot be the absolute possession of man. The information brought to us by the sciences, on the other hand, is fully and completely possessed; though this information is (of its nature) only a means; it never can satisfy us so that we desire it for its own sake. That which can satisfy us fully, and which we consequently desire for its own sake, is precisely what is given us in hope: 'the wisdom which is sought for its own sake', Aquinas says, 'is something which cannot become man's possession'; that wisdom, he goes on to say, is really only given to man in the form of a loan—*sicut aliquid mutuatum.*[18]

Philosophy, then, can only be said to 'possess' its object, to 'have' its proper object in the act of searching lovingly for it. That is a very important point, and one that is by no means universally accepted. Hegel, for example, seems to take special pains to contradict this conception of philosophy in the preface to the *Phenomenology of Spirit* where he tells us that his aim is to do what he can to enable philosophy to cease being called love of wisdom, and become real knowledge. That would be to formulate a claim that, in principle, goes beyond anything possible to man—a claim that occasioned Goethe's ironic dismissal of Hegel and philosophers of his sort with the words: 'these gentry think they lord it over God, Soul and World, though no one can comprehend what it all means.'[19]

The original meaning of the word philosophy, and its original implications too, contain a second idea that is only rarely given explicit appreciation. The legendary words of Pythagoras, the *Phaedrus* of Plato, and Aristotle, all contrast the *human philosophos* and the *divine sophos*.

Philosophy, then, is not the loving search for any kind of wisdom; it is concerned with wisdom as it is possessed by God. Aristotle actually calls metaphysics, the most philosophical part of philosophy, 'the divine science', because it deals with a wisdom that is only fully possessed by God.[20]

This second point, expressed in the original definition of philosophy, has more than one aspect. In the first place it emphasizes the notion that philosophy cannot fully comprehend its objects; the frontier that is here indicated is further defined as being the frontier between God and man: man can no more possess that particular wisdom than he can cease to be man. Furthermore, it means that philosophy implies a relation to theology; philosophy, if one may use the metaphor, is trained on theology, and this direction of thought towards theology is part and parcel of philosophy. The original conception of philosophy has a window open on to theology. And that, as everyone knows, is clean contrary to the current notion of philosophy. The decisive mark of modern philosophy on its own showing is that it has cut itself off from theology and has become entirely independent of faith and tradition. And there is a third point expressed in the original conception of philosophy: the refusal to consider itself a theology, a doctrine of salvation.

Now what is meant by 'wisdom as it is possessed by God'? The conception of wisdom underlying that phrase is the following: 'Wisdom can only be attributed without qualification to him who knows the highest cause'[21]—where cause does not, of course, mean simply, 'efficient cause', but implies 'final cause'.

'To know the highest cause,' then, does not mean to know the cause of some particular thing, but to know the cause of everything and of all things: it means to know the 'whither' and the 'whence', the origin and the end, the plan and the structure, the frame-work and the meaning of reality. It means to know 'the world' and its highest cause. Knowledge of this kind, in the sense of comprehensive knowledge, can only be possessed by God, the absolute Spirit. Only God can conceive the world as from a single point: as from himself as its one first cause. If 'wisdom can only be attributed without qualification to him who knows the highest cause', then in that sense, God alone is wise.

To be sure, the aim of philosophy is to understand reality as from a single principle. And essentially speaking, philosophy is 'on the way', *in via*, to this aim, loving, seeking and hoping, as we said, but at the same time too, incapable of attaining its aim. If we are to retain the original meaning of the word philosophy we must never forget to hold firmly to both parts of the definition.

Among other things, it can now be seen how this conception of philosophy makes a rationalistic interpretation of the world, deduced from a single principle, and from the first cause, quite simply inconceivable. In other words a complete and closed 'system' of philosophy is not possible. The claim to expound the world in a formula, or to have a formula with which to explain the world, is quite simply unphilosophic or pseudo-philosophy.

And yet Aristotle, in the *Metaphysics*, looks upon philosophy as the supreme science,[22] supreme because of its aim, because it aims at knowing the first cause of all things—even though its aim may only be attainable in the guise of hope or as a loan. In his commentary on this passage in the *Metaphysics*, Aquinas remarks that: 'The little that is won here (in metaphysics) weighs more than all that is won in all the other sciences.'[23]

It is because of the ambivalent structure of philosophy, because 'marvelling' sets one on a road that never ends, because the structure of philosophy is that of hope, that to philosophize is so essentially human—and in a sense to philosophize means living a truly human life.

IV

In the act of philosophizing, man's relationship to being as a whole is realized—he is face to face with the whole of reality; that was how we defined it. But long *before* the appearance of philosophy on the historical scene, from time immemorial, man has always had a given interpretation of the world and a meaning to attach to reality—'long before', 'from time immemorial'. This interpretation, this tradition, whether as teaching or as stories, was moreover concerned with the world as a *whole*.

'From time immemorial' man has been born into a doctrinal religious tradition offering an image of the world in its totality. An essential aspect of these traditions is that they existed and were valid 'from time immemorial'—long before any philosophy or interpretation of reality had been built upon experience.

Some theologians have held that these primitive traditions can be traced back to a first, original revelation, traced back to a communication granted to mankind 'in the beginning', to an unveiling of the meaning of the world as well as of the whole history of mankind, a proclamation submerged in myths, and encrusted with traditions belonging to all the races and peoples of mankind, but nevertheless still subsisting and living on. This is not the place to pursue this particular train of thought.

The important thing for our present purpose is to grasp that the great originators of Western philosophy, on whose thought it still largely lives, Plato and Aristotle, not only found and recognized a 'traditional' interpretation of the world alive and vigorous—they accepted it as their starting point when they began to philosophize. 'The ancients knew the truth, and if we were to discover it why should we bother with the opinions of man?'[1] And how often, elsewhere, Plato speaks of this or that doctrine as having been 'handed down by the ancients', and therefore as not only worthy of respect, but as unimpeachably and surpassingly true: in a word, as sacred. 'God, as the ancient doctrine tells us, holds the beginning, the end and the middle of all things in his hands, and leads them according to their nature and for the best', Plato writes in the *Laws*,[2] as an old man. And similarly, Aristotle, in the *Metaphysics*,[3] says that 'to us, who come afterwards, it has been handed down by our fore fathers and the ancients, that the whole of nature is surrounded by the divine.'

It is very important that it should be seen and understood that the great paradigmatic figures of Western philosophy are 'believers' in relation to an existing interpretation of the world, handed down by

148

tradition. It is important because, under the impulse of a rationalistic and 'progressive' doctrine, the history of philosophy as it has been written in modern times, does the exact reverse and sets the beginning of philosophy at the moment when thought cut itself free from tradition: philosophy, it is assumed, being the 'coming of age' of reason, of the *ratio*, and its emancipation from the tutelage of tradition. Rebellion against *religious* tradition is regarded as the very core of Western philosophy. And what is more, this is supposed to be clearly apparent from the history of of Greek philosophy: the pre-Socratics, the philosophers of Asia Minor, are looked upon as almost Voltairian figures fighting the battle of 'enlightenment', when in fact recent research tends to show that Homeric mythology (so sharply criticized by the pre-Socratics from Thales to Empedocles) was itself a sort of 'enlightened' theology, in opposition to which the pre-Socratics wished to return to a more primitive, 'traditional' pre-Homeric theology.

The first spring of Western philosophy, never to be recaptured, appears to show, on the contrary, that philosophy has always been preceded by a traditional interpretation of the world—a tradition which supplied the spark that set philosophy on fire.

But Plato goes even further. Not only does he say that there is a tradition 'handed down by the ancients', which ought to be honoured by anyone who philosophizes. He is also convinced that the 'wisdom of the ancients' is ultimately of divine origin: 'Knowledge came down to us like a flame of light, as a gift from the Gods, I am convinced, brought to us by the hand of some unknown Prometheus from a divine source—and the ancients, being better than we are, and nearer to the Gods, handed this tradition down to us.' That is what Plato says in the *Philebus*, in connection with the doctrine of ideas.[4]

According to Plato, 'wisdom, as it is possessed by God', had become known and accessible to us in some way or other, *before* our search for wisdom began: before man began to philosophize. Deprived of this prior counterpoint, of this divine wisdom that in some way or other enlightens us like a gift, prior to all our own efforts at thought—deprived of this counterpoint, philosophy considered as the loving search for 'wisdom as it is possessed by God' is utterly unthinkable—although, on the other hand, it is this very fact which expresses the independence and self-reliance of philosophy. That is to say, the independence of philosophy *vis-à-vis* what has always been said and revealed 'from time immemorial', i.e. the tradition that comes down from divine revelation, lies in the fact that philosophy begins by considering visible, concrete things and the realities of experience; begins from the bottom, questioning things that are met with in everyday life, that always seem more wonderful to those who are searching for wisdom, and always reveal new depths of wonder—whereas, what has already been revealed is essentially prior to experience and to experience assimilated into thought: it is *not* a 'result' wrung from experience, but a gift, something that has always been said.

This raises the question of the relation of philosophy to theology—theology in the large sense of the word, as the interpretation of that which is revealed. To simplify for a moment—though I do not think it is an over-simplification—the relation of theology and philosophy as it emerges in Plato and the whole of Greek philosophical thought comes more or less to this: Theology is always prior to philosophy, and not in a merely temporal sense, but with respect to inner origin and their relationship in that origin. Philosophical enquiry starts with a given interpretation of reality and of the world as a whole; and in that sense, philosophy is intimately connected, not to say, bound to theology. There is no such thing as a philosophy which does not receive its impulse and impetus from a prior and uncritically accepted interpretation of the world as a whole. It is in the field of theology, and quite independently of experience and previously to it, that the object of man's desire—'wisdom as possessed by God'—becomes visible, and it is this aim which supplies the impulse and guides the course of philosophical enquiry in its loving search as it moves through the world of experience.

That, however, does not mean to say that the theologian possesses what the philosopher is searching for.

In his distinctive capacity as the guardian and inter-
preter of tradition, the theologian does not, as such,
possess the knowledge of being characteristic of the
genuine philosopher. The revelation which teaches us
that the world is created by the Logos, is certainly a
statement that also concerns the whole structure of
reality; but the theologian whose business it is to preserve, defend and clarify the meaning of that statement
in the context of tradition as a whole, does not, by
that fact alone, acquire the worldly knowledge of the
philosopher that derives from the concrete consideration of the things of this world. On the other hand, the
philosopher who reflects upon the things of this world
in the light of the revealed doctrine of the Logos, will
attain to knowledge that would otherwise remain
hidden from him, though the knowledge he gains will
not be theological knowledge but demonstrable knowledge, philosophical knowledge of things in themselves.

The original concept of philosophy is characterized
by its freedom from prejudice *vis-à-vis* theology, at
least in so far as Plato is concerned. Plato would indeed
have been astonished had anyone asserted that he had
overstepped the limits of 'pure' philosophy and tres-
passed into the field of theology—in the *Symposium*,[5]
for instance, where Aristophanes is allowed to suggest
a grotesque, almost farcical origin of the sexes. The
first men, he says, were round, with four arms and four
legs, and double sexed; they were, he continues, subsequently cut in half (like pears ready for bottling)

152

and now consequently they are all in search of their 'other half', and this impulse is the essence of Eros, 'the desire and pursuit of the whole'. But in spite of its farcical details, the fundamental structure of this story is that in the beginning our nature was healthy and unimpaired; but in course of time man was driven by 'hybris', by the consciousness of his great powers and still 'greater thoughts', to trespass upon the divine. As a punishment for this overweening pride, for wishing to be like Gods, men lost their original perfection, their completeness, though they were left with hope: Eros is the desire of man to recapture his original state of perfection, and perhaps the power which really will fulfil this desire—'if we honour the Gods'.

That is undoubtedly not philosophy, nor is it a 'result' which could be reached by thought alone and the experience of reality. But is it not, because Plato ponders the question 'what is Eros, ultimately?', at the same time allowing full weight to the answer given by religious tradition—is it not, perhaps, because of this conjunction of philosophy and theology (so characteristic of the Platonic dialogue), that to read him is to experience something intimately concerned with man? Is that not really the source of the universal appeal of the dialogues, and the reason why they answer so completely to the whole of man's nature?

And consequently, it is impossible to pursue a philosophy that is consciously and radically divorced from theology—and at the same time invoke the name of Plato. To philosophize in the manner of Plato, or with any claim to continue the tradition of Plato, can only be done upon a theological ground base and with a full consciousness of that counterpoint. No one can seriously enquire into the cause of all things (and that is what happens in philosophy), and for the sake of arbitrary methodical tidiness, simultaneously exclude the existing religious tradition where it touches upon these basic themes—unless they no longer accept the account given by tradition. What cannot seriously be done, is to accept tradition, believe it, and then set it aside in order to philosophize.

The question then naturally arises, where nowadays the legitimate pre-philosophical tradition is to be found. What is the present-day form of what Plato[6] calls 'the gift of the Gods, brought down to us by some unknown Prometheus'? The answer to that question is that since the extinction of the classical world, there exists no pre-philosophical tradition relevant to the world as a whole, except the Christian tradition. There is no theology in the Western world of today, unless it be the Christian. Where, indeed, is there such a thing as a non-Christian theology, in the full sense of the word?

This means to say that if the claims and the requirements of Plato are to be honoured, in the Christian aeon, philosophy can only be pursued as the counterpoint to Christian theology. 'How is a Christian philosophy possible?' is a far less difficult question to answer than the question 'How is a non-Christian philosophy possible?'—assuming, always, that we understand by philosophy all that Plato understood by it.

Obviously, this does not mean that a man has only to be a Christian, or to accept the Christian tradition, in order to become a philosopher without further ado —for that means, after all, to enquire deeply into the nature of things, and is linked to a man's vision of the world and dependent on his natural genius. Nor should this be understood to mean that the only vital philosophy is a Christian philosophy. One can also philosophize vigorously in opposition to Christianity: but Christianity can only be replaced or supplanted, in this respect, by another belief, however carefully it may be decked out as purely 'rational' —for rationalism has its own creed. And in that case, the structure of philosophy, as Plato understood it, as the counterpoint to faith, is still retained. (Where the religious tradition has entirely dried up and words like God, Logos, Revelation no longer convey any meaning, philosophy ceases to be possible.)

The life and soul of philosophy, and the tension that goes with it, depend upon its retaining what I have called its contrapuntal relation to theology. That is where it strikes root and where it draws the salt of the existential. If Heidegger's philosophical work has had such a stimulating effect, it is because philosophy had become a shrivelled-up, intellectual discipline, the preserve of specialists in the worst sense of the word, and had lost all touch with theological themes (this was partially true even of so-called Christian philosophers). The explosive character of Heidegger's philosophy on the other hand is simply due to the fact that it asks challenging questions, and his questions are challenging because their source and impetus is theological, and so too should their answers be—though it is true that the theological answer is flatly rejected by Heidegger. But quite suddenly, once again, one could taste the salt of theology on one's tongue.

The same thing is happening nowadays in France to an extent and in a sense that is no mere fashion: 'existentialist' atheism is by no means a 'pure' philosophy, nor is it even 'scientific': it is a theological position and brings to philosophy an essentially theological dimension—so that although it is not of course any more true, since it is concerned with a pseudo- or anti-theology, it is quite certainly more vital and deeply concerns the real man in us—because it is concerned with the whole, which is how we defined philosophy.

'Atheistical existentialism', writes Jean-Paul Sartre, 'concludes from the non-existence of God that there is a being which exists and is not defined by any higher will than its own: that being is man'—and nobody, surely, will accept that as a philosophical thesis and not as a theological thesis, an article of faith even. But it does force thought and thinker on to the theological plane; and that is the type of counterpoint that makes for vital, vigorous philosophizing.

On the other hand, to be vital and true, philosophy must be the counterpoint to a true theology, and that, *post Christum natum*, means Christian theology. But to repeat, that does not mean to say that philosophizing allegedly referring to Christian theology is automatically vital and true. What it does mean is this: a philosophy at once vital and true either does not come into existence at all—and it is perfectly possible that we shall have to wait in vain—or if it does arise then it can only be a Christian philosophy —in the above sense.

That is not—need I say—a philosophical statement. But it is, nevertheless, one with a genuine philosophical background and implies a philosophy which (ever since the beginning) has been understood as the loving search for 'wisdom, as it is possessed by God'. Moreover, the nature of the philosophical act inevitably involves overstepping the frontier of 'pure' philosophy which is anyway only theoretically and methodologically definable, and not existentially separable: it is conceptually distinct but does not correspond to any real and distinct field. One cannot, in fact, philosophize without taking up a theological position. One cannot do so because philosophizing is a fundamentally human relationship to reality and is only possible if our whole human nature is involved —and that necessarily involves the adoption of a definite position with respect to ultimate things.

This attempt to answer the question 'what do we mean by philosophizing?' would not be complete without a brief reference to the notion of a Christian philosophy, though of course with no sort of claim to exhaust that many-sided problem or even to throw light on its main outlines.

To begin with, it is very necessary to contradict the widely held opinion that Christian philosophy, (or 'a' Christian philosophy) can be distinguished from a non-Christian philosophy by the fact (among other things) that a Christian philosophy is ready with all the answers. That is not so. Although Christian philosophy takes shape as the counterpoint to unquestioned certainties, it is Christian philosophy which most fully grasps and expresses a truly philosophical sense of 'wonder', with its source in ignorance. One of the great thinkers of our time, whose thought is inspired by Aquinas, has written that the characteristic of Christian philosophy, its distinguishing mark if you like, is not that it has all the answers up its sleeve, but that more than any other philosophy, it is inspired by the sense of mystery.[7] Even in the sphere of theology and of faith it is not after all true—in spite of the *certainty* of faith—that everything is clear to the believer and every problem already solved; on the contrary, as Mathias Joseph Scheeben said, the

truths of Christianity are in a very special way inconceivable; the truths of reason are generally inconceivable; but the distinguishing mark of the truths of
Christianity is that 'in spite of being revealed, they still
remain hidden'.[8]

Someone might well ask, at this point, where the
advantage of Christian philosophy lay, by comparison with a non-Christian philosophy, if it does not
succeed in providing a full and adequate solution, if
it does not hand one out the answer, and if the problem and question still remain. Perhaps, after all, the
greater *truth* lies in seeing the world in its real character as a mystery, and as unfathomable. Perhaps reality
is more truly and more profoundly apprehended when
we experience being as a mystery, and as something
which cannot be grasped in the hand in an all-embracing answer, or by means of some transparent
and marvellously clear system. And that is the claim
of Christian philosophy: to be truer—in its very recognition of the mysterious character of the world.

The consequence of this is not, indeed, to make
philosophizing simpler. It appears, moreover, that
Plato must have known and experienced that fact
—if it is true to maintain[9] that he called philosophizing
tragic *because* whoever philosophizes is always forced
back upon myths, *because* no 'purely' philosophical
interpretation of the world could ever be complete
and pursued to the point at which it formed a perfectly
closed circle.

Christian philosophy is not, in fact, less intellectually arduous because, as one might be tempted to think, faith 'illumines' reason. If it reaches back to theological arguments (as it does in the philosophy of Aquinas for example), that is not a way of making ready answers possible but a way of breaking down methodological barriers in order to give the most genuine philosophical impulse, the loving search for wisdom, a wider field—a way of introducing it into the realm of mystery, a realm which is by definition boundless, and to enter into that infinite realm is to enter on a path along which one can continue for ever without coming to an end.

On the other hand, the point of these theological truths about the world as a whole, and the meaning of human existence—one aspect of the function of theology in our salvation—is that it should hinder and resist the natural craving of the human spirit for a clear, transparent and definite system. That is what is meant by the old phrase that the truth of faith is the 'negative norm' of philosophical thought.

This is not the way, in fact, to make philosophizing 'simpler'. Quite the contrary; no one could really suppose that it could be otherwise, and the Christian philosopher's task is more difficult than that of a thinker who does not feel himself bound by the truths of faith handed down by tradition. Something of this problem is felt in Hölderlin's *Hyperion* where he says: 'Heart's wave could not curl and break beautifully into the foam of spirit, unless the ageless silent rock of destiny stood in its path.'

It is the ageless, silent, immovable rock of revealed truth that hinders and prevents philosophical thought from flowing on uninterruptedly in the lifeless calm of a well-constructed channel. The complexity necessitated by this impediment is one of the distinguishing marks of Christian philosophy. For instance, a philosophy of history that reckons with the dominion of Antichrist at the end of time, with the fact that, humanly speaking, the history of mankind ends with a catastrophe, and in spite of this is not a philosophy of despair—a Christian philosophy of history in fact, cannot possibly end in an intellectually simple view of history; whereas the philosophy of 'progress' becomes so simple (though one can no longer say that it is obvious!)—precisely because it omits the Apocalypse.

No, philosophical thought does not become simpler merely because one can cling to the norm of Christian revelation. But—and this claim is self-evident to the Christian—a Christian philosophy is truer and does fuller justice to reality. The opposition which revealed truth provides, the impediment it puts in the way of philosophical thought, is a fruitful opposition. The claim to which the Christian philosopher submits is a severe one. One of the distinguishing marks of Christian philosophy is that it places itself under compulsion to endure that stress and strain, and is thus carried beyond the sphere of purely intellectual difficulties. It is a more complex task because it rejects formulae that are clear and plausible *at the cost* of leaving things out, or of ignoring or selecting from reality. The contemplation of revealed truth is a disturbing element in Christian philosophy though a very fruitful one, for it means that the framework of philosophy is widened, and, above all, it can never rest satisfied with the flat, one-dimensional 'harmonies' of rationalism. That is the moment when a Christian philosophy, striking upon the rock of divine truth, foams and boils; and that is its unique privilege.

Christian philosophy, then, is enriched by its contrapuntal relation to the truth of revelation. In this, we are assuming two things (as a *condicio sine qua non*); first of all that the *Christian* character of the philosophy in question is genuine and powerful, and secondly (this is so often overlooked by Christians) that its *philosophical* character is genuine and powerful. (Maurice de Wulff's well-known history of medieval philosophy ends with the words that Scholasticism did not die from lack of ideas, but from lack of men!)

And so in this sense the 'No' that theology opposes to philosophical thought, the effect of theology as *norma negativa* is anything but 'negative'. For surely no one could describe as purely negative the fact that thought, from the very outset, is prevented from falling into certain errors. The positive aspect only fully emerges in the fact that through the recognition of revealed truth, the human mind grasps certain philo-

162

sophical truths though 'in themselves' they could be
attained and established by natural means. The statement that 'states without justice are simply robber-
bands' is certainly intelligible to natural reason, and
yet it is no mere chance that it should not occur in a
work on the philosophy of law but in a theological
work, St. Augustine's *The City of God*.

The question may now perhaps be asked, whether,
after all we have said, philosophy is not really entirely
superfluous for the Christian. Is not theology enough,
or just simply faith? 'Those who have a *Weltan-
schauung* and who are determined in no circumstances
to relinquish it', Windelband says in his *Introduction
to Philosophy*[10] (and what he says certainly applies to
the Christian), 'have no need whatsoever of philosophy.' Now of course it is quite true that our salvation
does not require us to philosophize; only one thing is
necessary, and it is certainly not philosophy. The
Christian does not and cannot await an answer from
philosophy on the subject of his salvation, nor, of
course, salvation itself. And so he cannot philosophize
as though his salvation depended upon his understanding of the world. To lose oneself in philosophical
problems, to identify oneself existentially, as it were,
with them, though characteristic of all personal, independent philosophizing—and the more earnest and
genuine the enquiry, the more characteristic it will be
—is really foreign to the believer. It sometimes seems
as though Aquinas's conviction that such a thing as

'a comprehensive understanding' of *anything* in the world is impossible, were tinged with delight and almost with humour.

Philosophy is as necessary and as superfluous as the natural perfection of the human being. As we saw, to philosophize is to realize the natural bent of the human mind and spirit towards the whole. But who could possibly calculate the precise degree of that necessity in individual cases?

And now one final thing: up till now we have spoken as though 'Christianity' meant doctrine, statement, truth exclusively. We have spoken of the Christian philosopher in much the same way as one might speak of a Kantian philosopher—by which is meant someone whose philosophy is in agreement with that of Kant. But to say that a man is Christian in the act of philosophizing does not mean that his point of view is that of Christianity considered as doctrine. For Christianity is essentially reality and not merely doctrine. The problem before a Christian philosophy does not therefore lie in harmonizing natural and supernatural knowledge theoretically; nor does it consist in the choice of the method to be adopted to that end. The point is that a man's existence should be so deeply rooted in the Christian reality, that his philosophy, too, should become, as a result, Christian. 'The philosophy a man choses', Fichte said, 'depends upon the sort of man he is'—not an altogether happy way of expressing the thought, since that is not how things happen (one does not after all chose a philosophy as one would choose assorted chocolates). Still, what Fichte meant is clear enough, and very much to the point. Even where natural knowledge is concerned, the discovery of the truth is not merely a matter of hard thinking, and when the truth concerns the meaning of the world, a good brain is not enough: the whole human personality is involved.

Now, to be a Christian *is* a qualification of being, of the whole of a man's being, and the more he opens himself to it, the more completely will it inform and transform all his faculties, including his intelligence. This is not the place, nor is it my business, to speak in detail of these things. What has been said should be enough to show everyone something of the existential structure of a Christian philosophy. In Thomas Aquinas[11] we find a distinction, which sounds altogether modern, between two ways of knowing: between properly theoretical, conceptual knowledge, knowledge *per cognitionem* on the one hand, and knowledge *per connaturalitatem* on the other, knowledge based upon the relations in being. The first form gives one knowledge of something foreign, in the second form one knows what belongs to one. A moralist for instance, who is not necessarily a morally good man, judges the good in the first manner; a good man knows what goodness is in the second, *per connaturalitatem*— on the basis of a direct participation, of an inner sympathy, and the unerring scent of love, for it is love, as,

165

likewise, Aquinas[12] goes on to say, which brings about *connaturalitas*, which makes something foreign into one's own.

Now, to speak with judgment about divine things in this manner, as of one's own, is only possible to him who, in the words of Denys the Areopagite, 'is not only learned in the divine, but who has suffered it'.[13]

The undiminished form of Christian philosophy will therefore only be realized by one who has not just 'learnt' his Christianity, to whom it is not just 'doctrine', with which his conclusions are brought into theoretical and conceptual agreement—but by one who lets Christianity become real in him, and this makes these truths his own, not by knowledge alone, but through 'suffering' and experiencing reality, the Christian reality—and then philosophizes on the meaning of life and the natural reasons and causes of the world.

NOTES

I

1. Commentary on *Proverbs*, 4 d. 26, 1, 2.
2. M. Heidegger, *Was ist Metaphysik?* p. 22. (Frankfort, 1943.)
3. Blake.
4. Commentary on the *Metaphysics*, 1, 3.
5. *Protagoras*, 318 f.
6. *Theaetetus*, 174.
7. *Phaidon*, 59.
8. *Symposium*, 172 f.
9. Newman, *Idea of a University*, V, 6.
10. Aquinas, ibid., 1, 3.
11. Newman, ibid.
12. *Novum Organum*, 1, 3; 1, 81.
13. *Discours de la Méthode*, 6.
14. Aquinas, *Quaest. disp. de veritate*, 2, 2.
15. Gregory the Great, quoted by Aquinas, ibid.

II

1. *Der unsterbliche Geist in der Natur*, p. 63 (1938).
2. Ibid., p. 76.
3. Uexküll-Kriszat, *Streifzüge durch die Umwelten von Tieren und Menschen*, p. 40.
4. *Die Lebenslehre*, p. 131.

5. *De anima*, 3, 8 (431 b).

6. *Quaest. disp. de veritate*, 1, 1.

7. *Summa Contra Gentes*, 3, 112.

8. *Quaest. disp. de veritate*, 2, 2.

9. See Josef Pieper, *Wahrheit der Dinge* (1948).

10. *Summa Theologica*, I, 76, 5 ad 4.

11. *Quaest. disp. de potentia Dei*, 5, 10 ad 5.

12. *Quaest. disp. de virtutibus cardinalibus*, 1.

13. *Meno*, 85, 81.

III

1. *Theaetetus*, 175.

2. Ibid., 155.

3. Eckermann, 18 Feb. 1829.

4. 2. 69.

5. Windelband, *Einleitung in die Philosophie*, p. 6 (1923).

6. *Quaest. disp. de potentia Dei*, 6, 2.

7. *Summa Theologica*, I, ii, 32, 8.

8. *Rhetoric*, 1, 2.

9. *Summa Theologica*, I, ii, 32, 8.

10. *Summa Contra Gentes*, 4, 33.

11. Ibid.

12. *Symposium*, 204.

13. Commentary on the Apostles' Creed.

14. *Summa Theologica*, I, ii, 31, 5.

15. Dilthey's letters to Count Paul Yorck von Wartenburg 1877–1897, p. 39 (Halle 1923).

16. *Phaedrus*, 278.

17. Commentary on St. John's Gospel.

18. Commentary on the *Metaphysics*.

19. In a letter to Zelter, 27 Oct. 1827.

20. *Metaphysics*, 983 a.

21. *Summa Theologica*, II, ii, 9, 2.

22. *Metaphysics*, 983 a.

23. Commentary on the *Metaphysics*, I, 3.

IV

1. *Phaedrus*, 274.

2. *Laws*, 7, 15.

3. *Metaphysics*, 1074 b.

4. *Philebus*, x, 16.

5. *Symposium*, 189 f.

6. *Philebus*, 16.

7. Garrigou-Lagrange. *The sense of Mystery and the clair-obscur of the Spirit*.

8. M. J. Scheeben, *Die Mysterien des Christentums*, p. 8 (1941).

9. G. Krüger, *Einsicht und Leidenschaft*, p. 301 (1939).

10. P. 5.

11. *Summa Theologica*, I, 1, 6; II, ii, 45, 2.

12. *Summa Theologica*, II, ii, 45, 2.

13. Dionysus Areopagitica, *De divinis nominibus* 2, 4, quoted by Aquinas, *Summa Theologica*, II, ii, 45, 2.